AFTER MIDNIGHT

By the same author

CHURCH AFLAME

AFTER MIDNIGHT

by

PAUL B. SMITH, B.A., F.R.G.S.

Associate Pastor of The Peoples Church, Toronto

Foreword by
TORREY M. JOHNSON, M.A., D.D.

Introduction by
J. EDWIN ORR
Th.D., D.Phil. (Oxon)

London
MARSHALL, MORGAN & SCOTT
Edinburgh

LONDON
MARSHALL, MORGAN & SCOTT, LTD.
33 LUDGATE HILL, E.C.4

AUSTRALIA & NEW ZEALAND
317 COLLINS STREET
MELBOURNE

SOUTH AFRICA
P.O. BOX 1720, STURK'S BUILDINGS
CAPE TOWN

CANADA
EVANGELICAL PUBLISHERS
366 BAY STREET
TORONTO

THE PEOPLES PRESS
100 BLOOR EAST
TORONTO

U.S.A.
SWORD OF THE LORD PUBLISHERS
WHEATON, ILL.

First published in 1956

MADE AND PRINTED IN GREAT BRITAIN BY PURNELL AND SONS, LTD.
PAULTON (SOMERSET) AND LONDON

To

CAPTAIN DONOVAN J. JOWRY

whose friendship has made
this book possible

FOREWORD

What we need in the evangelical movement throughout the world today is literature that is as fervent and tender as our finest evangelistic and revival preaching.

Young converts and more mature saints who have been touched with new fire from the pulpit need that same kind of fire on the printed page. *After Midnight*, which is a volume of the best thought and preaching of Rev. Paul B. Smith, fills just such a need.

New converts will find food for their souls and new assurance of their salvation as they read the pages of this fine volume. Pastors and evangelists will not only find profitable preaching material but will feel the spirit of Paul B. Smith pulsating upon every page. More mature Christians will want to pass this book on to unsaved relatives and friends after they have read its pages.

Paul B. Smith who is the son of the world-famous evangelist and missionary statesman, Dr. Oswald J. Smith, radiates in this volume the evidence of the large anointing of the same spirit which has rested upon his father, a real man of God.

As these sermons have been preached from the pulpit by Paul B. Smith, hundreds have been led to Christ. As these sermons are read in this volume throughout the English speaking world, other hundreds will be won to Jesus Christ.

DR. TORREY M. JOHNSON.

Chicago, Ill.

INTRODUCTION

It was my privilege to enjoy the assistance of the Reverend Paul Brainerd Smith when he first started to serve God in public ministry in his late teens. It would be trite to say that I have since been interested in his ever developing ministry. Rather I rejoice in his proven usefulness in three continents. He has retained the dynamic punch of his early preaching, but matched it with a maturity of thought and presentation which enables him to step into the first rank of evengelists throughout the world.

I have found his message *After Midnight* deeply moving, and the same can be said of others of his messages included in this book. Alas, I have not had the opportunity of reading or hearing all of them. Yet I consider it a privilege to write this word of introduction of the man and his message.

There has always been the possibility of a preaching son being overshadowed by his famous father, in this case Dr. Oswald J. Smith of Toronto. But Paul Smith has made his own way, and is better known in some parts of the world than is his father, which is saying something. His recent campaigns in New Zealand were extraordinary, as I learned passing through Auckland this year.

Many people who have not heard this able young evangelist will want to read his messages. The publishers are therefore assured of a wide market, and the readers of a real blessing.

J. EDWIN ORR.

CONTENTS

CHAPTER I

AFTER MIDNIGHT

FROM THE BIBLE

"Then shall the kingdom of heaven be likened unto ten
virgins, which took their lamps, and went forth to meet
the bridegroom. And five of them were wise, and five were
foolish. They that were foolish took their lamps, and
took no oil with them: but the wise took oil in their
vessels with their lamps. While the bridegroom tarried,
they all slumbered and slept. And at midnight there was
a cry made, Behold, the bridegroom cometh; go ye out to
meet him. Then all those virgins arose, and trimmed
their lamps. And the foolish said unto the wise, Give us of
your oil; for our lamps are gone out. But the wise
answered, saying, Not so; lest there be not enough for us
and you: but go ye rather to them that sell, and buy for
yourselves. And while they went to buy, the bridegroom
came; and they that were ready went in with him to the
marriage: and the door was shut. Afterward came also the
other virgins, saying, Lord, Lord, open to us. But he
answered and said, Verily I say unto you, I know you not.
Watch therefore; for ye know neither the day nor the
hour wherein the Son of man cometh."[1]

[1] Matt. xxv. 1–13.

CHAPTER I

AFTER MIDNIGHT

THE word midnight occurs only fourteen times in the entire Bible. It is always used in connection with some outstanding demonstration of the power of God, either in salvation or judgment. There is only one exception where the word occurs in a casual sense.

The first time the word midnight appears in the Bible is in the Old Testament account of the inauguration of the passover feast among the children of Israel. It was midnight when God sent the Death Angel to destroy the first-born in the homes of the Egyptians and it was midnight when the Death Angel passed over the homes of the children of Israel, sparing them because of the blood that was sprinkled on the door-posts of their houses.

It was midnight when Samson took the doors and the gate-posts of the city of Gaza and carried them to Hebron, demonstrating once again the power of God in his life through his own deliverance from a trap that would have meant certain death.

It was midnight in the jail at Philippi when Paul and Silas sang praises unto God and His power was demonstrated by an earthquake which resulted in their liberation and the salvation of the Philippian jailer.

It was midnight when the Apostle Paul performed his greatest miracle. He was giving his farewell message to the people of Troas in an upper room on the first day of the week. He had begun to preach at the time of the evening meal and apparently was still going strong at midnight. One young man by the name of Eutychus fell asleep at the midnight hour and tumbled out of the window. The Bible says he was taken up dead. It was then that Paul wrought a miracle that restored life to him.

Thus the word "midnight" is very significant throughout the entire Bible. It is used in a casual sense only once and everywhere else in connection with some outstanding incident resulting in a demonstration of God's power either in salvation or in judgment. It is the pivot point of the story of the ten virgins recorded in the twenty-fifth chapter of the Gospel of Matthew.

I wish to answer three questions about midnight as it occurs in this passage: What is the meaning of the word here? What will happen to the people of the world who stay out after this midnight? What can cause the midnight hour to strike in a man's life?

In the usual sense of the term, of course, the word midnight refers to that point of time that marks the end of one day and the beginning of another. Midnight usually marks the end of the activities of the majority of the righteous people in the world and the beginning of the activities of the majority of the unrighteous people of the world. It marks the end of the working day for most law-abiding citizens and the beginning of the working period for most outlaws and criminals. Even in common usage, the word midnight generally signifies an end and a beginning.

There are a great many events that can be considered midnight hours in a very real sense—hours that mark a very definite end to one part of our lives and the beginning of another part. There is the midnight that strikes within the heart of every mother when, for the first time, she says good-bye to her child and sends him off to school with the other boys and girls. For five or six years he has been a baby—loved, protected, nourished, and cherished by his parents. Now he is a baby no longer. Babyhood has ended and boyhood has begun. There is a very poignant midnight in the heart of the average mother or father when that transition takes place.

There is a midnight that comes into the life of the school-boy on the day of graduation. It is a time that marks the end of school days and the beginning of college or working days. As he approaches his graduation the student realizes that all he has wanted to do, everything he has been anxious to accomplish during his educational career, has either been done or it will never be done. Midnight has struck. It has ended that period and ushered him into another sphere of life.

There is the midnight that occurs in the life of the older man as he reaches the years of his retirement. He is forced to look back upon the early days of his life. He remembers, perhaps, the dreams and aspirations of his youth—the things that he longed to accomplish in life. Now as he starts the final treck down the other side of the hill he knows that his dreams have either come true or they will never come true. His aspirations have either been realized or they will never be realized. His work has been accomplished or it will never be accomplished. Midnight has struck. Working days are ended and retirement has begun.

I am not thinking now, however, in terms of any of these other midnight hours that come into the lives of men and women. The midnight about which I am desperately concerned is that hour which is spoken of in the twenty-fifth chapter of Matthew. These other midnights of life are important, but God's midnight is the most solemn, the most serious, and the most important midnight that will ever strike in any man's life. It is the midnight that marks the end of man's opportunity to get right with God and the beginning of his eternity either with God or without God.

This is the one midnight in life that is absolutely inevitable and inescapable. Just as surely as your heart beats and the blood flows through your veins, some day there will strike in your life that midnight hour which will end your opportunity of getting right with God and will begin your eternity either saved or lost.

Now we come to the second question of our subject: What will happen to the people of the world who insist upon staying out after God's midnight? If you will read the story of the wise and foolish virgins carefully, you will find the answer to that question in the Bible. The five foolish virgins tried to get in to the wedding feast after midnight and the Bible says, "the door was shut,"[1] and there is no reason to believe that it was ever opened again.

When I was a boy in the city of Toronto we always had a ruling in our house that when we went out on any given day we were supposed to come back the same day. If we managed to get home before midnight, the door was always open; but if we arrived after midnight, the door would be closed and locked. Any time before midnight we simply opened the door and walked in. No explanation was necessary; but if we came after midnight, we would be forced to knock on the door or ring the bell until we had roused someone in the house. Then some sort of an account was demanded. The thing that impresses me about my boyhood days is the fact that no matter how late I stayed out I could always eventually awaken someone and the door would be opened. But, as I read my Bible, I learn that such is not the case with God's midnight. The Bible makes it clear that when the midnight hour strikes on God's clock in any man's life the door of opportunity is shut and shut forever.

The five foolish virgins were not shut out because they had no invitation. They had received exactly the same

[1] Matt. xxv. 10.

invitation as the five wise virgins. They knew all about the wedding feast. They were fully aware of what was required of them, but the Bible declares that they were shut out despite the fact that they had been invited.

The five foolish virgins not only had the same invitation as those who got in, but they had the same intentions. The most surprised people in the world were these five foolish girls that found themselves shut out after midnight. They had expected to be there. They had intended to go. They had been looking forward to the wedding feast, but they were shut out despite the fact that they intended to get in.

There was only one reason—they came too late. They had failed to take time to make the necessary preparations for the wedding feast, and when the midnight hour struck they were found unprepared. Afterwards they came, but afterwards was too late.

What a tragedy it is that there are so many people who have received invitation after invitation to accept the Lord Jesus Christ as their own personal Saviour who will some day be shut out of Heaven along with the heathen world that never had even one invitation! How terrible to think that scores of men and women, who have lived their lives intending some day to get right with God, will find themselves barred from Heaven along with the multitudes who never gave salvation a second thought.

If ever there is a day when you find yourself separated for eternity from the presence of God, remember that it will not be because you did not have an invitation, nor will it be because you did not expect some day to be saved. It will be because you stayed out after midnight.

The final question of our subject is the most important: What can cause midnight to strike in a person's life?

The Second Coming of Christ would cause midnight to strike in a man's life if he should be alive at that time.

Some generation of human beings will be living in this world when Jesus Christ comes back again. It may be the next generation. It may be a generation that will live several hundred years from now, or it could be this generation. There is no point in trying to avoid the issue, for the Bible declares in absolutely unmistakable terms that some day the Lord Jesus is going to break through the gloom of this old world and come back to take His Church to be with Him.

The Word of God is filled with it. One out of every thirty verses is related to it. For every once that His first advent is mentioned His second advent is mentioned eight times. There are entire chapters and whole books that are given over completely to the truth of the second coming of the Lord Jesus Christ. It is foretold in the Old Testament and emphasized again and again in the New Testament.

"I go to prepare a place for you. And if I go and prepare a place for you, I will come again, and receive you unto myself; that where I am, there ye may be also." [1]

"For the Lord himself shall descend from heaven with a shout, with the voice of the archangel, and the trump of God: and the dead in Christ shall rise first: then we, which are alive and remain, shall be caught up together with them in the clouds." [2]

"Ye men of Galilee, why stand ye here gazing up into heaven? this same Jesus, which is taken up from you into heaven, shall so come in like manner as ye have seen him go." [3]

That day is coming—perhaps very, very soon. When it comes, it will be midnight in the life of those who live to see it. Their chance to get right with God will be gone and it will be gone forever. Those who have accepted

---

[1] John xiv. 2-3   [2] I Thess. iv. 16-17.

[3] Acts i. 11.

Jesus Christ as Saviour will be taken to be with Him. Those who have continued to reject Him—those who have remained outside the ark of safety until after midnight—will be left. Then, as the judgment of God begins to fall upon the world, those who have been left behind will flee to the mountains and the caves and cry out in desperation for the rocks to fall on them and hide them from the wrath of the Lamb.

Jesus could return today, and if He should, midnight will have struck for the entire world. Your opportunity to get right with God will be gone.

The second event which could cause midnight to strike in a man's life is his own death. When his heart ceases to beat and his blood ceases to flow and the breath has gone from his body, his chance to turn to God will be at an end.

There are some who have already passed the "three score years and ten"[1] mark of life. They have already gone beyond their prime and the grave is in view. They realize, as perhaps others in the world fail to realize, that their time is short. Others are already in the grip of some fatal disease and they know, and the doctors know, that it is only a matter of time until it will be all over.

Whether you are old or young, whether you are well or gripped by disease, you are living in the "valley of the shadow of death."[2] You are journeying through that sphere of time which God has cut out of eternity in which death has jurisdiction and at any moment may claim you as his victim.

Some day you must die. It could be any time. It might be today. The only time that really belongs to you is the immediate present. Next year belongs to God. Next month belongs to God. Tomorrow belongs to God. The next hour of your life belongs to God. The only time that is yours is now. The only time that you can make decisions is now. The only time at which you can accept

[1] Ps. xc. 10.   [2] Ps. xxiii. 4.

Christ is now. You control the "now" of your life. God controls the future.

That is why the Bible says, "Now is the accepted time; behold, now is the day of salvation."[1] That is why God warns each of us: "Boast not thyself of tomorrow; for thou knowest not what a day may bring forth."[2] In this age of war, accident, and sudden death, we might well read that verse: Boast not thyself of *the next hour*, for thou knowest not what a *moment* may bring forth.

If you fail to accept Jesus Christ as your Saviour now, there may be no tomorrow. Once death has claimed you as his victim, your opportunity to get right with God will be over. Midnight will have struck and you will be outside.

There is one more thing that could cause midnight to strike. The second coming of Christ may not take place in this generation and therefore may not affect it. It may be that a man has many more years of life in this world. However, man can cross the midnight dead-line himself by rejecting Christ too many times.

Almost every evangelist, pastor, and Christian worker can recall cases of men and women who had many opportunities to accept the Lord Jesus Christ, but continually rejected Him, and finally seemed to arrive at the place in their lives where it became impossible for them to respond.

Here is what happens. The first time a person hears the Gospel, his heart is strangely stirred. There is a pungent spirit of conviction that moves him God-ward. The Spirit of God is wooing him towards the Lord Jesus Christ. Everything within him seems to be urging him to accept the divine invitation. It would be the easiest thing in the world for him to do so, but for some reason, that first time he resists the convicting power of the Spirit of God, and although it is a struggle for him to do so, he says his first

[1] 2 Cor. vi. 2.   [2] Prov. xxvii. 1.

"No" to Jesus Christ. It is hard to reject; it would be easy to accept.

The next time he hears the Gospel, again there is a great spirit of conviction upon him. Again the Spirit of God is working in his life. Again everything within him seems to urge him forward. Again it would be easy to close in with God, but again he yields to the dictates of Satan within his life, and says, "No." But now it is a little easier to reject and it has become a little more difficult to accept.

Again and again he hears the Gospel. There is the struggle of the soul. The Spirit of God convicts. Satan draws the other way. But down through the years he refuses to reverse his decision until now it has become very easy to say, "No," and it is growing increasingly difficult to say, "Yes." It is a simple matter now to resist the working of the Spirit, and it would be difficult for him to yield.

As long as a man continues to resist the working of the Spirit of God he is building up a wall of resistance around his own heart that will eventually become so strong and so calloused that it will be impossible for him to change. When that day comes, he will have said "No" for the last time, and never again will he say "Yes."

I do not believe that the Spirit of God draws a dead-line in the life of any man, but I am thoroughly convinced that a man can draw the dead-line for himself by a continual rejection of the Lord Jesus Christ.

"But," you say, "how do I know but that already I have said my final 'No' to God? Maybe I have already drawn the dead-line of opportunity across my life. It could be that my heart has become so hard and calloused and indifferent to the pleading of the Spirit of God that it would be impossible for me to relent and turn to God even now. How can I tell when the dead-line is drawn?"

Is your heart stirred? Is there any interest at all? Is

there the least evidence of the convicting power of the Spirit of God? Are you concerned in any way about your soul's salvation? If so, then you have not crossed the dead-line. As long as there is interest, as long as there is concern, as long as there is any sign of anxiety whatsoever, it is not too late for you.

The Bible still reads, "Whosoever shall call upon the name of the Lord shall be saved."[1] If you have enough interest today to call upon Him for salvation, you can be saved. The Bible says, "Him that cometh to me I will in no wise cast out."[2] If there is enough concern on your part to come, you will not be cast out. God will accept you and will make you His child. But let me urge you to call upon the name of the Lord *now* that you may be saved. Come to Him *now* that He may make you His child, lest even as this message goes forth you reject Him as Saviour, say another "No" to God, and in doing so draw the dead-line across your own life which will cause midnight to strike and leave you outside.

Some day your opportunity to get right with God is going to end. Whether you are ushered into an eternity of blessedness, joy, and satisfaction in His presence, or whether you are cast into outer darkness where there will be weeping, wailing, and gnashing of teeth, will depend upon the decision which you make before midnight.

There is a day of harvest, but there is a day when the harvest ends. There is a summertime of opportunity, but there is a time when the summer will be past. God grant that you may not stay out until after midnight and have to cry out in desperation from the darkness of an eternity with the doomed and the damned in hell, "The harvest is past, the summer is ended, and we are not saved."[3] God grant that you may get in before midnight.

[1] Acts. ii. 21.   [2] John vi. 37.
[3] Jer. viii. 20.

CHAPTER II

THE SINS THE BIBLE NAMES

FROM THE BIBLE

"And the scribes and Pharisees brought unto him a woman taken in adultery; and when they had set her in the midst, they say unto him, Master, this woman was taken in adultery, in the very act. Now Moses in the law commanded us, that such should be stoned: but what sayest thou? This they said, tempting him, that they might have to accuse him. But Jesus stooped down, and with his finger wrote on the ground, as though he heard them not. So when they continued asking him, he lifted up himself, and said unto them, He that is without sin among you, let him first cast a stone at her. And again he stooped down, and wrote on the ground. And they which heard it, being convicted by their own conscience, went out one by one, beginning at the eldest, even unto the last: and Jesus was left alone, and the woman standing in the midst. When Jesus had lifted up himself, and saw none but the woman, he said unto her, Woman, where are those thine accusers? hath no man condemned thee? She said, No man, Lord. And Jesus said unto her, Neither do I condemn thee: go, and sin no more."[1]

[1] John viii. 3–11.

CHAPTER II

THE SINS THE BIBLE NAMES

"JESUS stooped down, and with his finger wrote on the ground, as though he heard them not."[1]

You will notice that Jesus wrote twice on the ground, and in between the first time and the second He said something. He wrote, He spoke, He wrote, and they went out.

There has been a great deal of discussion as to what Jesus wrote on the ground. As far as we know, that was the only time Jesus ever wrote anything. Strangely enough, He only wrote twice on the ground, and yet there have been more books written about Him than any other one person that has ever lived. I think I know what He wrote the first time, and I think I know what He wrote the second time. I do not believe that He simply idly placed letters or words in the sand. I believe the writing of Jesus in the sand had something very specific to do with the occasion at hand. The writing of Jesus in the sand had something to do with the woman, and the writing of Jesus in the sand also had something to do with the Pharisees and the scribes which had asked Him the question.

There before Him with head bowed was a woman that had been brought by a group of self-righteous religious men. The woman had committed a great sin, and Jesus did not mitigate the seriousness of her sin. As everybody looked on and as the woman was bowed there, I am

[1] John viii. 6.

convinced that the very first thing He wrote was the name of her sin—*adultery*. I think that when they saw that the crowd gathered a little closer because they were interested in seeing the woman condemned. They were pleased with Jesus. He was dealing with the sin of this woman and eagerly these religious people came a little closer and watched.

Then, I think, Jesus went on, without saying a word, and wrote *fornication*. They all nodded their heads. Then He wrote the word *theft* and they gathered a little closer still. He wrote the word *drunkenness* and the habitual loafing drunkard on the outskirts of the crowd saw it and turned away quickly. He was convicted by what Jesus wrote. Then came the word *liar*, and the scribes and Pharisees closed in, but two or three people on the edge of the crowd began to drift away. That was getting too close to home. He wrote the word *blasphemy*, and again the scribes and Pharisees nodded their heads and gathered closer. One of them reached down and picked up a stone, ready to stone the woman. Finally, He wrote the word *idolatry*, and the crowd was one hundred per cent behind Him, agreeing with everything.

He had named the sins of the world: adultery, fornication, theft, drunkenness, lying, blasphemy, idolatry. That is the list of the sins of the world. These people that had brought the woman to Jesus were thrilled. Apparently He agreed with their code of action. It seemed that Jesus was absolutely in sympathy with what they were going to do.

Then Jesus stopped writing and He turned to them and He said this: "He that is without sin among you, let him first cast a stone at her."[1] The Scribes and Pharisees saw the list of sins on the ground and they were not guilty of any of them; they were a religious crowd. They were not

---

[1] John. viii. 7.

guilty of those sins any more than most of the people who attend our churches today are guilty of them. They did not know the meaning of those sins in their own personal lives. Those things had never been a problem to them. Because they were a religious group of people they were not convicted when Jesus wrote the names of those sins on the sand. At last when Jesus said, "Let him that is without sin among you first cast a stone at her,"[1] every one of them reached down, picked up a stone, and were about to hurl it at the woman when they noticed that Jesus was writing again.

Do you know what I think He wrote the second time? I believe that opposite the word *adultery* He wrote the word *covetousness*, and the oldest Pharisee was pricked to his heart. He dropped his stone, he bowed his head, and he walked away. Without saying anything, beside the word *fornication* Jesus wrote the word *pride*, and a slightly younger man, an arrogant sort of fellow, a man that thought himself better than the common crowd, was convicted by the Spirit of God because Jesus had struck home to his own heart. He too dropped his stone, bowed his head, and with tears running down his face he walked away. Right opposite the word *theft* Jesus wrote the word *jealousy*. Three or four more left. Opposite the word *drunkenness* He wrote the word *anger* and half a dozen left.

Then in quick succession under the words *lying*, *blasphemy*, and *idolatry* Jesus wrote *disobedience* and *extortionism*. By the time He had written the final word the last of those who had accused the woman were gone, convicted by their own conscience, and she was left alone with Jesus.

Sins are named in almost every book of the Bible. You can find consolidated lists in such passages as Mark 7,

[1] John viii. 7.

1 Corinthians 6, Galatians 5, Ephesians 4, Colossians 3,
1 Peter 2, and Revelation 21. The books of Psalms,
Proverbs, and Moses are filled with the names and des-
criptions of things which are sins in the eyes of God.

If you were to go through your Bible very carefully
and put down the name of every sin which is mentioned
from Genesis through Revelation, it would take several
large pieces of paper and you would have to write with
very small letters to condense them even in that space.
However, if you analyse the various sins that are mentioned in the Bible, you will discover that there are only
seventeen basic sins. All of the other names for sin can be
included under one of these seventeen names.

There are three varieties of sin. There is sin which will
be judged by God. There is sin which will be judged by
God and for which a man will be ostracized by society,
and there is sin which will be judged by God, for which a
man will be ostracized by society, and for which he will
be put into jail. If you were to make a list of these sins in
their various categories under the headings Imprisonment,
Ostracism and Judgment, it would look something like
this:

Imprisonment	Ostracism	Judgment
1. Illicit sex relation-ships	1. Lust	1. Covetousness
2. Murder	2. Lying	2. Pride
3. Theft	3. Idolatry	3. Hatred
4. Drunkenness	4. Blasphemy	4. Disobedience
5. Slander		5. Unbelief
		6. Envy
		7. Anger
		8. Extortionism

The thing we must be careful to notice is this: According to the Bible, all sin is condemned by God. "The wages

of sin is death."[1] The Bible does not say the wages of certain kinds of sin is death. It says unmistakably that the wages of sin—any variety of sin—is death. "The soul that sinneth, it shall die."[2] Again God does not limit spiritual death to one kind of sinner. He says the soul that sinneth—in any way—shall die.

"There is no difference."[3] This means there is no difference between men. "For all have sinned, and come short of the glory of God,"[4] but if it means this, it also means there is no difference in the sins that men commit. Sin is sin in the eyes of God and sin results in the judgment of God.

All sin is condemned by God. The sins that we have listed under the word "social" are not only condemned by God, but if a man commits these sins he will be ostracized by society. The sins that we have listed under the word "imprisonment" bear a threefold penalty. If a man commits these, he is judged by God, ostracized by society, and put into jail.

I am very much aware of the fact that I am bringing this message to a group of people who would never be convicted if I were to talk about the sins for which people are put into jail. I also realize that the majority who read this would not be convicted if I were to preach about the sins for which a man is ostracized by society. This message is reaching a group of religious people who live a comparatively moral and upright life. If the Spirit of God is going to reach the hearts of men and women such as this, He must convict them on the level of life at which they live, and so I want to talk about the sins for which men will never be put in jail or ostracized by society, but which the Bible clearly says are some day to be condemned by God.

[1] Rom. vi. 23.
[2] Ezek. xviii. 4.
[3] Rom. iii. 22.
[4] Rom. iii. 23.

Pride is one of these sins. The dictionary definition of pride is this: "A high opinion of ourselves that causes us to disdain others." There are several different kinds of pride. There is social pride. That is the feeling of disdain that lies in the hearts of men and women who move in a certain social set for those people who live in a lower social bracket. Social pride not only makes us happy that we move in our social bracket but it causes us to "look down our social nose" at anybody who lives in a lower social bracket. This is social pride, and pride is sin in the eyes of God.

Then there is business or economic pride. That is a feeling of superiority and disdain as a result of our financial standing. Not only are we proud of the fact that we are in a particular financial position but we disdain and refuse to associate with anyone who cannot measure up to our level. This is business pride, and pride is sin according to the Bible.

Scholastic pride is rampant throughout this country, especially among our college and university students and graduates. Some of us feel that because we have attained to a certain academic standing we have a right to look down upon anyone who has not had the opportunity of education that has been ours. This is scholastic pride, and pride is sin.

Many parts of the Christian world are seething with racial pride. Racial pride causes one group of people to despise another group because they belong to another race. Racial pride makes one country feel that their race is superior to that of another country. This is racial pride, and pride is sin.

Pride involves two things—happiness because we belong to a certain group and disdain for anyone who belongs to an inferior group.

Hatred is another sin which the Bible names right along

with murder, illicit sex relationships, and idolatry. The dictionary definition of hatred is: "A dislike that wishes evil on another." Hatred is the feeling that makes us cross the street to avoid coming into contact with someone whom we dislike. Hatred makes us happy when the person we dislike gets into trouble. Hatred causes us to refuse to speak to someone else or have fellowship with them, and hatred, according to the Bible, is sin.

Very common among nominal Christian people is the sin of jealousy, and again we need to remember that jealousy is listed right along with the great sins against society that are named in the Bible. God does not distinguish between murder and jealousy. He does not point out any difference between adultery and jealousy. Jealousy is sin in the eyes of God. The dictionary tells us that jealousy is "a feeling of pain at another's good luck or success." Envy, of course, is simply a variety of jealousy. It is jealousy over someone else's success plus a desire that his success could be ours. Jealousy is what makes people loath to admit the fact of another's good fortune. Jealousy makes us say, "He does well—but." Jealousy makes some of us glad when somebody fails in an endeavour. Jealousy is what causes professing Christians to sit around the table after an evangelistic service and criticize almost every Christian worker about whom they can think. It is that thing that creeps into Christian conversation and drives people to point out defects in the life, character, or methods of a man who obviously has done a great job for God. This is jealousy, and jealousy is sin.

Anger is another of the sins which the Bible names and which some day will be judged by God. Anger is "a vexation of spirit as a result of direct or indirect personal injury." Wrath is simply a more extreme form of anger.

There are two kinds of anger—the kind that explodes and the kind that sulks. There is the anger that boils over suddenly and there is the anger that simmers on for days. They are both exactly the same, but they are manifested in different forms. Anger is passed over much too lightly in the majority of our Christian circles, because anger, according to God, is sin. Anger is sin just as lying is sin. Anger is sin just as blasphemy is sin. Anger is sin just as fornication is sin. Anger is sin in the eyes of God.

We could go on and talk about some of the other sins that are named in the Bible, but these are enough for our purpose. The Word of God tells us that "Whosoever is born of God doth not commit sin."[1] The most generous interpretation of this passage that we can give is this: "Whosoever is born of God doth not practise sin." This means that if a man is a child of God, he is not a habitual sinner. He does not continue in sin. He does not practise sin.

Suppose in the course of an evangelistic campaign the pastor were to come to me with a problem something like this: "There is a very fine Christian gentleman in my congregation. As a matter of fact, he is one of the officials of the church. He is an untiring worker, loyal to the church, and faithful to God. He has only one shortcoming. Every once in a while he murders somebody—a fine man otherwise, but he cannot seem to stop committing murder. What should I do about him? What does he need? How can I help him?"

Without a moment's hesitation, I reply: "What that man needs is to rededicate his life to God. He needs to learn the lesson of victorious living. I will preach a sermon on the deeper life and we will pray together that he will make a decision and reconsecrate his life to the Lord Jesus Christ."

If I were to answer in such a manner, anyone who knows his Bible would be forced to say that I had made a

[1] I John iii. 9.

mistake. What that man needs is not rededication but re-generation. He does not need to learn the lesson of victorious living. He needs to accept the Lord Jesus Christ as his own personal Saviour and have the miracle of the new birth wrought in his life. If he had committed murder only one time, we might conclude that it was a mistake; we might think he had slipped; we might assume that he was not actually living up to his deepest convictions, but when he goes on murdering indefinitely we must conclude that he has never been born again. And why? "Because whosoever is born of God doth not *practise* sin."[1]

Here is another instance. The pastor comes to me with this problem: "There is a very fine elderly lady who sings in our choir. She has been with us now for over twenty years—a great Christian character and a zealous worker in the church, but she has one weakness. She is an unmitigated liar. Every once in a while we find her out in a lie. What should we do about it? How can we help her? What does she need?"

Does this lady need to rededicate her life to the Lord? Does she need to learn the secret of victorious living? Is it reconsecration that she lacks? Of course not! Absolutely no! If I have only a casual knowledge of the Word of God, I will know that such a woman has never been born again. She has never been regenerated. She has never passed from death unto life. If she had lied once, it might be excusable. It might be considered a slip. We might assume that she had made a mistake, but if she had proved herself to be a habitual liar, then the only conclusion to which we can come is that she has never been born into the family of God. And why? Because "Whosoever is born of God doth not *practise* sin."

[1] 1 John iii. 9.

c

The two cases that I have cited, of course, are hypothetical. The incidents have never happened to me and undoubtedly have never been experienced by any other Christian worker. However, very often the visiting evangelist is confronted with another problem. The pastor comes to him with this kind of story: "I have two men in my church. Both of them are fathers of lovely families. They are diligent in their service to God and their work for the church. They possess untiring energy and unflagging zeal, but for at least ten years they have refused to have fellowship with each other. Many years ago there was a division over some personal issue and as far as I know they have not spoken to one another from that day to this. They hate each other thoroughly. They have created a division in the church. Some of my people follow the leadership of one of them, the rest follow the other. What am I to do? What do they need? How can we help them?"

Or perhaps it is another problem. "There is a fine young woman who teaches in our Sunday School, but her spirit is spoiled with jealousy. She hates to see anyone else in a prominent position. She sulks if she is left out of anything. She is constantly vying with everyone else for attention. Unless she is the centre of attraction, she is unhappy, and this has been going on for many, many months. How can we solve the problem? What can we do? Is there any way we can help her?"

Here is another example: "There is a young man in my church who is invaluable to the work of the church but he spoils his testimony constantly with his uncontrollable temper. At almost every church meeting he flies off the handle and loses control of himself. This has happened not once, or twice, but again and again. He cannot seem to gain the victory over his anger."

And so we could go on with problems that every pastor

faces month after month. Our usual answer to such questions is reconsecration, rededication, or the victorious life. But are we answering the question correctly?

I am well aware of the fact that pride might dominate in the life of a man once or twice. Hatred could be victorious on rare occasions. Covetousness might get a grip now and then. Jealousy could have sway under pressure once in a while. Sometimes anger might rule, but at great intervals. But when these things reoccur again and again in the lives of men and women who claim to be the children of God, what must we conclude? There is only one conclusion. The man who commits these sins habitually has never been born again. He does not need teaching on victorious living. He does not need to re-dedicate his life to God. He needs the miracle of the new birth wrought in his life. He needs to be saved. And why? "Whosoever is born of God doth not *practise* sin."[1]

If a man is born again, he does not practise murder. Everyone agrees with that. If a man is born again, he does not practise lying. Everyone says "Amen." If a man is born again, he does not practise pride, hatred, covetousness, jealousy or anger. These are the sins which the Bible names and these are the sins which the Christian does not practise. If he does, he is not a Christian. He has never been born of God.

The Word of God says, "If any man be in Christ, he is a new creature: old things are passed away; behold, all things are become new."[2] I believe that this verse means exactly what it says. The Christian is a changed person. The Christian has a transformed character. The Christian is a new creature. "Old things have passed away, and all things have become new."

Sometimes I meet people who claim that there has never been any real change in their lives. They were

[1] 1 John iii. 9.   [2] 2 Cor. v. 17.

reared in Christian homes. They have always associated with Christian people. They have always been familiar with the Word of God, and when they made a decision there was no real change. What they were after their conversion was just about the same as what they were before.

Whenever I meet a person such as this, I am reminded of the fact that Jesus said, "I am come to call sinners to repentance."[1] Repentance is an intrinsic part of salvation. The man who has never repented has never been saved. Without repentance there is no salvation, and repentance involves a definite transformation of personality and character. I believe that there is a change of life that makes a different boy or girl even out of a child that has always lived in a Christian home. "If any man be in Christ, he is a new creature."[2]

The reason we have so many people in our churches who claim to be Christians but whose lives indicate that they have never been born again is that it is possible for people to be converted without ever having been regenerated. You can be converted to a great many things.

For instance, some people are converted to a church. They attend a church which has an evangelistic emphasis, where the music is bright and cheerful, and they enjoy the service. They decide to move from their own church to this church. They have been converted, but there has been no repentance. There has been no salvation. There has been no regeneration. They have simply been converted to a form of worship.

Some people are converted to an evangelist. They are drawn by the magnetic personality of a man, and they make a decision—a very definite decision—but it is a decision to follow a man. There have been no tears of repentance. There has been no conviction of sin. There

[1] Matt. ix. 13.　　　　　[2] 2 Cor. v. 17.

has been no renunciation of sin. There has been no acceptance of Jesus Christ as Saviour. There has been conversion. There has not been regeneration. They have been converted to a man, but they have never been regenerated by God.

Others are converted to a praying mother. They know that for years their Godly mother has been crying out to the Lord for their salvation. Conscious of this fact, sometime in their lives they decide to join the church. Perhaps they raise a hand, walk down an aisle, or go into an inquiry room. They make a decision, And why? Because they are convicted of their sin? No! Because they wish to repent of their sin? No! Simply because they wish to please a mother whom they love. They have been converted, but they have not been regenerated.

Some are converted to a sweetheart. Here is a young man who is keeping company with a Christian girl. He knows that unless he becomes a Christian she will not marry him, and so he makes a decision. He makes a profession of faith. He walks an aisle, kneels at an altar, or goes into an inquiry room. But what has taken place? Has he been regenerated? Has he been born again? Has a miracle taken place in his life? Of course not! He has been converted to the desires of a sweetheart. He has never been regenerated as the result of conviction of his own sins.

Thus, our churches are filled with men and women who have been converted but who have never been regenerated, and in the lives of these people it is little wonder that the sins we have mentioned crop up habitually.

The only conversion that saves is the conversion that results in regeneration. Man must see his sin. He must be convicted of his sin. He must repent of his sin. He must come to the Lord Jesus Christ and accept Him as his own personal Saviour. Then, and only then, does the Holy

Spirit of God work in his life the miracle of the new birth. Then, he becomes a regenerated soul.

Everyone agrees that the man or woman who practises illicit sex relationships, murder, theft, drunkenness, or slander is not a Christian. Everyone agrees that people who practise lust, lying, idolatry, or blasphemy have never been born again. Most of us, however, fail to realize that men and women who practise covetousness, pride, hatred, disobedience, unbelief, envy, anger, or extortionism are committing sins that are just as much sin in the eyes of God as these other things, and some day they will be judged by God. The man or the woman who commits these things habitually is obviously not a Christian. He has never been born again because, "Whosoever is born of God doth not *practise* sin"[1]—sin of any kind.

The woman caught in the act of adultery was brought to Jesus. She was a sinner. They knew it. She knew it, and Jesus knew it; but Jesus made it absolutely clear that the people who brought her were also sinners. She was guilty of adultery. They were guilty of jealousy, hatred, pride, envy, etc. Both were sinners in the eyes of God, because "There is no difference."[2]

After the others had been convicted by what Jesus wrote and had left, the woman found herself alone with Jesus. She confessed her sin and then heard His words, "Go, and sin no more."[3]

[1] I John iii. 9. [2] Rom. iii 22.
[3] John viii. 11.

CHAPTER III

WHY WORRY ABOUT HELL?

FROM THE BIBLE

"And if thy hand offend thee, cut it off; it is better for thee to enter into life maimed, than having two hands to go into hell, into the fire that never shall be quenched: Where their worm dieth not, and the fire is not quenched. And if thy foot offend thee, cut it off: it is better for thee to enter halt into life, than having two feet to be cast into hell, into the fire that never shall be quenched: Where their worm dieth not, and the fire is not quenched. And if thine eye offend thee, pluck it out: it is better for thee to enter into the kingdom of God with one eye, than having two eyes to be cast into hell fire: Where their worm dieth not, and the fire is not quenched."[1]

[1]Mark ix. 43-48.

CHAPTER III

WHY WORRY ABOUT HELL?

SOME years ago there was widespread interest and terrible confusion created in the city of Toronto concerning the Bible truth about Heaven and hell. The subject received front-page publicity in our daily newspapers as a result of a statement made by a renowned British clergyman in the preaching mission he was currently conducting. Here is what he said in answer to the questions of a number of young people about life after death:

"I am a bit horrified at the number of young people who send me in questions on what I think about Heaven and hell. I think it is quite disgraceful for young people to be bothering about Heaven and hell at their age. It is a form of escapism. Religion is something to make them different here and now. They should be following Christ in their daily lives now, and not worrying about Heaven and hell either for themselves or their friends. I am sure there is a hell on earth. Basically, hell is to be the child of God and be without God. A lost child who desperately wants his father and cannot find him is desperately miserable. That's what hell is. Whether there is a hell as a state after death is a question upon which Christians differ."

This is but one of many similar statements about the life after death that were flaunted before our people—confusing the minds of the unsaved and shaking the confidence of some of our weaker Christians. I want to answer the question of my subject from the Word of God: "Why Worry About Hell?"

Let me say, first of all, that in this message I intend to use very, very plain language. I do not believe there is any necessity for soft-pedalling, or dodging the issue, or trying to find words that make the subject sound nice. This is not a nice subject; this is not a thrilling subject; this is not a pleasant subject to discuss, and so there are no nice words that we can use with which to discuss it.

I am reminded in this connection of a minister who was a little afraid to use the Bible words about future punishment, and in his message on the subject he said something like this, "If you do not love the Lord Jesus Christ, you will be sent to that place which it is not polite to mention." Let us be logical. For instance, if I were to see a house on fire across the street, would I say, "I believe the operation of combustion is proceeding yonder"? Of course not. If the house across the street was on fire, without a moment's hesitation, without trying to find fancy words, or nice words, or interesting words, or pleasant words with which to describe it, I would simply run down the street and cry out at the top of my lungs, "FIRE! FIRE!" and everybody would know exactly what I meant.

As I talk about the place of punishment, I am going to use the words that Jesus used. When I talk about hell, I am going to use the vocabulary of Jesus; and because the Bible speaks in this manner, I make absolutely no apology for doing likewise.

This is not a theological discussion about hell, and for that reason I am not going to take time to talk about the various words that are used to describe the places of future punishment—both in the Old Testament and in the New Testament, in the Hebrew and the Greek. It is sufficient to say that the hell about which we are talking, and the hell about which the Lord Jesus Christ spoke all the way through the New Testament in His earthly ministry, is the place which is the last abode of all wicked people—the hell that is the final destination of the sinner.

The British clergyman's thesis, of course, was this: If we make absolutely sure that we are right in this life, then it follows that we will be right in eternity. If we concentrate upon preparing for this world then automatically we will be prepared for the next world. In other words, take care of time and eternity will take care of itself. Therefore, the question of our subject—"Why Worry About Hell?"

The thesis that I wish to set forth, on the other hand, is the direct converse of this. It is my firm conviction, and I believe it is the firm conviction of the majority of Bible-believing Christian people, that the emphasis of the Word of God is *not* upon time but upon eternity; *not* upon the "here" but upon the hereafter; *not* upon this world, but upon the next world. We believe that the Bible declares, in unmistakable terms, the importance of getting ready for eternity, the importance of escaping the wrath of God, and the importance of preparing for Heaven. The only inference we can draw from the Word of God is that if we are adequately prepared for the life hereafter, we cannot help but be prepared for the life that is here now. If we are ready to live in the world that is to come, we cannot but be ready to live in the world that is.

Notice what the Bible has to say about life—how short, how uncertain, how unimportant: "Our days on the earth are as a shadow, and there is none abiding."[1] Or again, "My days are swifter than a weaver's shuttle, and are spent without hope."[2] Or again, "For what is life? It is even a vapour, that appeareth for a little time, and then vanishes away."[3]

It is possible, you see, to be prepared for life, and yet not be prepared for eternity. However, it is not possible

[1] I Chron. xxix. 15. [2] Job. vii. 6.
[3] Jas. iv. 14.

to be prepared for eternity and not be prepared for life. You can quite easily be prepared for this world and not be ready for the next world. But if you are ready for the next world, then you cannot help but be ready for this world.

It follows that if we believe the next world is the most important, that eternity should have the pre-eminence over time, and that what is to come hereafter is more important than what is to come now, then we cannot help but worry about hell, and seek to do everything within our power to "flee from the wrath to come,"[1] and make our position in Heaven secure.

I wish to answer four important questions about hell, and in answering these questions I believe that it will be apparent to everyone who is honest with himself and honest with God why everybody—young and old alike—should worry about hell.

Why should there be a hell?

There should be a hell for at least two reasons, if not more. In the first place, man's sense of justice demands that sin should not go unpunished.

Again and again, as we live and look about us in this world, we are forced to see the great deficiency of moral balance. We see the wicked prosper and the righteous deprived. We see men scraping down into the dregs of depravity and seeming to pay no price for it, while others, who live morally and above-board, oftentimes are forced into difficulty after difficulty, heartache after heartache, and sorrow after sorrow. The drunkard thrives, the harlot is secure, the blasphemer prospers, and the murderer goes unpunished. The liar gets away with it, the thief lies in luxury, the atheist seems to be blessed, and the degenerate lives and dies in peace.

[1] Matt. iii. 7.

We see the broken-hearted girl-mother bearing the burden of her shame and suffering alone, while the brute who ruined her moves in his circle of friends as before; but even as we see it, our sense of justice rises up and clamours for recognition, as it cries out that there must be a day coming, as surely as there is a God in Heaven, when justice will be done.

Dr. Harry Ironside, the late Pastor of the great Moody Memorial Church, in Chicago, tells this story: A young man had married a very beautiful young woman. They became the parents of a sweet little baby girl, but even as the new little life breathed her first breath her young mother breathed her last. The baby grew up, nourished and cherished by the father, who saw in her the very replica of his wife. She became the focal point of his existence, the object of all his dreams and aspirations. But one day, after many years, a young man came into their home who succeeded in winning the affection of that young woman, and upon doing so basely deceived her, lured her into grievous sin, and after ruining her young life he cast her off, a broken-hearted girl.

That father had been a Universalist, but when the poor girl came sobbing, broken-hearted, seeking her father's house after weeks of wandering, during which she had been afraid to go home, and told him what had happened, and when he saw the wreck that had been made of the idol of his heart and life, he exclaimed with an oath, "If God Almighty hasn't a hell for fiends like the one who has wrecked my happiness and ruined my child, He ought to make one!"

And from the heart of every decent human being comes a loud "Amen." Deep down within our souls we seem to know that sin, some day, must be punished. Wrong, somehow, must be righted. Justice, somewhere, must gain the victory, and so—even without the Bible—as we look upon the sin and the ruin, the blasphemy and debauchery, the depravity and degradation of human beings, our hearts and our minds and our better selves say with the man in the story, "There should be a hell."

But not only does our sense of human justice demand that sin be punished: the Bible declares, in decisive terms, that sin *will* be punished; there will be a day of reckoning; there will be a final settlement; wrongs will be righted. Sin has its wages, and some day the wages of sin must be paid. "For whatsoever a man soweth," the Bible says, "that shall he also reap."[1]

Man cannot sow blasphemy and reap blessing. He cannot sow debauchery and reap delight. He cannot sow lying and reap laughter. He cannot sow murder and reap a mansion. He cannot sow sin and reap salvation. He cannot sow hell and reap Heaven. "For whatsoever a man soweth, that shall he also reap."[2]

Some day the drunkard must pay; the harlot must pay; the liar must pay; the blasphemer must pay; the sinner must, and *will*, pay the terrible price of his sin.

> *Three men went out one summer night,*
> *No care had they, or aim,*
> *And dined and drank. "Ere we go home,*
> *We'll have," they said, "a game."*
>
> *Three girls began that summer night*
> *A life of endless shame,*
> *And went thru drink, disease, and death*
> *As swift as racing flame.*
>
> *Lawless and homeless, foul they died;*
> *Rich, loved and praised, the men:*
> *But when they all shall meet with God—*
> *And justice speaks—what then?*[3]

[1] Gal. vi. 7. [2] Gal. vi. 7.
[3] Written by Oswald J. Smith, Toronto, Canada.

The voice of human justice cries out that there must be a hell. The Word of God declares, in terms that cannot be mistaken, that there will be a hell.

What is hell?

Let me answer by saying two things about hell. First of all, hell is the everlasting death of both the soul and the body of the sinner in everlasting fire.

Now in order to substantiate this statement, I must prove five things: first, hell is a place to which the soul goes. Second, hell is a place to which the body goes. Third, hell is a place where both soul and body are destroyed. These first three facts can be gathered from many different verses of Scripture, but one is sufficient. Notice the words of Jesus, and notice them very, very carefully. There is no ambiguity whatsoever. Jesus says, "Fear him which is able to destroy both soul and body in hell."[1]

We see, then, that hell is a place to which the soul goes, but not only is it a place to which the soul goes, it is also a place to which the resurrected body of the sinner goes. Not only is it a place to which the soul and body of the sinner go, but it is a place where soul and body will be destroyed. In other places in the Bible this destruction is called a death. To be cast into hell, the Book of Revelation tells us, means to pass into the second death.

Finally, I must prove from the Word of God that hell is a place of fire that is everlasting. Of course, all through the Bible, in almost every instance where hell is described, it is compared to some form of fire. We find words like these: "hell fire,"[2] and "the lake of fire burning with brimstone."[3] We are warned, furthermore, that the fire is everlasting. Hell, declares God's Word, is a place where "their worm dieth not and the fire is not quenched."[4]

[1] Matt. x. 28.
[2] Mark ix. 47
[3] Rev. xix. 20.
[4] Mark ix. 48.

Not only is the fire of hell everlasting, but the Bible states that the punishment, or the death, or the destruction that the fire of hell inflicts is also everlasting. "These shall go away into everlasting punishment."[1] Thus, we see that hell is a place where body and soul suffer the pangs of an everlasting death.

If we could, somehow—even for a moment—catch a vision of what death for the sinner involves (I am speaking now of the death that will eventually separate him from this world and usher him into the next world), if we could get a vision of the agony and the pathos and the awfulness of the sinner's first death, and then to that picture add the one word *everlasting*, we might have some conception of what it would mean to go to hell.

Death, even to the Christian, is not a beautiful thing. Although he knows that beyond the shadow lies the sunshine, and beyond the valley looms the mountain-top. Although deep within his heart he knows that to die means to be with Christ, and it is far better, yet inbred in the very fibre of that same heart, even for the Christian, there is the human fear of death that comes like a clammy hand to tear at the heart and cause the entire body to shudder and the mind to cringe.

Nobody likes to die! But for the sinner, how much more terrible must be the throes of death. Think of the thoughts and memories that must plague his dying mind. Helpless upon his last bed, he casts his eye back, perhaps, over the panorama of life and considers what he has been. He hears the church bells of every Sunday ringing again and he remembers the many times he has broken the Lord's Day. As he tosses from side to side he recalls the many sermons he has heard, the many warnings he has had, and how they have all been rejected.

During those fleeting hours, as death is creeping on,

[1] Matt. xxv. 46.

gradually yet surely usurping the place of life, memory becomes very strong. It has an uncanny clarity of vision, as with a lightning flash it brings before the dying sinner the long-forgotten years of his childhood: the earnest exhortations of a Godly father, in whose arms, one day, as an innocent babe, he had been carried up to the altar and dedicated to God. Twisting and turning on his sick bed, he seems to hear the sobbing of a fond mother as she used to kneel by his bedside and, bathing the covers with her tears, cry out to God for his salvation. I can conceive of no one entering hell with a worse grace than the man who goes there with his mother's tears on his head, and with his father's prayers following him at his heels.

Yes, in those dying hours for the sinner memory brings back everything, but to the sinner it is no fountain of joy, but rather:

> *Remembrance wakes with all her busy train,*
> *Swells at his breast and turns the past to pain.*

It tells him of all the sins he has committed. It reminds him of the things which he had hoped were forgotten; those sins committed in the glare of broad daylight, that sin committed behind closed doors in the darkness of the night. Oh God, what agony it must be to a dying sinner, simply to look back on all his sins!

Memory is no liar. Glancing back on the record, it seems to cry out, "Look! Look at the love you have slighted; at the solemn warnings you have ignored; at the opportunities you have deliberately wasted." As the miserable man lies there, convulsed with his pain, memory seems to stick daggers into his conscience, crying out, again and again, "It shall be more tolerable for Tyre and Sidon at the day of judgment, than for you."[1]

And in those dying moments the sinner is further

[1] Matt. xi. 22.

D

tormented as he realizes that he has to leave all of his earthly joys forever. There he lies, struggling for breath, his heaving lungs panting for air, forced to take one last fleeting look at the joys of this life, knowing that he shall never experience another.

He sees the harlot, that dirty toy of dirtier men, with whom he has spent the nights of his debauchery and revelry. The rich man looks upon his broad acres, or zooming profession, or gigantic business enterprise, and knows he must leave it all forever. Yes, in his dying, grating, gasping breath he is torn asunder by the realization that now, at last, "the harvest is past, the summer is ended,"[1] and he is not saved.

His mind, that has gone beyond the power of making decision, gathers together enough stimulation from the searing agony of death to tell him that the voice that once, with arms outstretched, said, "Come unto me, all ye that labour and are heavy laden, and I will give you rest," will soon say, "Depart from me, ye cursed, into everlasting fire, prepared for the devil and his angels."[2]

Death comes, the eyes are staring from their sockets, the throat is dried up like the desert sand, the death rattle gurgles the overture, and the jarring, jolting symphony commences—and it never ends, for out of one death the sinner is ushered into another death, the second death—the death that lasts forever. The sheet has been pulled over his eyes, the body is still, but out in eternity the blanket of God's wrath has enshrouded him in the everlasting destruction of soul and body in hell.

The first death has finally conquered. One woe is past; the spirit leaves the body, hoping that its trials are over, until coming out of the "bourne of space and time" and into the confines of another world he meets a commissioning angel, with bared sword, who cries out, "One

[1] Jer. viii. 20.   [2] Matt. xxv. 41.

woe is past; and, behold, there come two woes more hereafter."[1]

This is hell—everlasting death—a dying, with all of its agony, that goes on for ever. How else can I describe it? How can I picture the pain, the weeping, the wailing, the gnashing of teeth? There is no pain on earth great enough to be compared to the pains of hell. Napoleon, a man who was supposed to have had the hardest of hearts, one day rode across the battlefield. As he rode, his horse stepped on a poor, wounded man, just about to die, and in his dying breath the wretched soldier rose up and gasped. Whereupon Napoleon cried out in horror, "Oh God, what pains a man may suffer!"

Could you and I put our ear to the entrance of the world of spirits for a moment and listen to the cries of the damned, we too would turn back with countenance blanched and cry, "Oh God, what pains a man may suffer!"

Could all the misery that has ever horrified the staffs of our hospitals be gathered together, it would not convey the least conception of the pains of those who are doomed to dwell in eternal fire and everlasting burning. Body, mind, and spirit—all will be tormented; each one racked on a bed of fire; every fibre strained to its utmost; every nerve made a highway for the searing feet of pain. Even Jesus Christ, the most compassionate of all preachers, preached the most awful hell. He called it a place "where their worm dieth not, and the fire is not quenched."[2]

But notice in the second place: Not only is hell a place of everlasting death for soul and body, but hell, the Bible tells us, is a place where there is absolutely no hope.

Do you remember what happened to the man who came to the feast without the wedding garment—descriptive, of course, of the sinner in the story that Jesus tells in the twenty-second chapter of Matthew? The King says this

[1] Rev. ix. 12.   [2] Mark ix. 48.

to his servants, "Bind him hand and foot, and take him away, and cast him into outer darkness; there shall be weeping and gnashing of teeth."[1]

Hell is a place, then, of outer darkness, a place where there is absolutely no light. Where there is no light, there is no hope. In this life there is always hope. Here is a man whose business is ruined, but within his heart is the hope of a come-back. Here is a woman whose husband is on the brink of death, but there is ever the hope that the crisis may be past and recovery begun. Yonder is one whose body is being eaten away with cancer, but there is a faint glimmer of hope that, ere he dies, the cure will be found. On earth there is always hope, but in hell there is no hope.

Those who have gone to hell do not even have the hope of dying, or the hope of being annihilated. They are forever—forever—forever lost. On every chain of hell there is engraved *forever*. In the flames is blazed out the word *forever*. Above their heads they read *forever*. On all sides of them they hear *forever*. Their eyes are seared and their hearts are sick at the thought that it is *forever*. Oh, if I could tell you that hell would some day burn out and that those who were lost might be saved, there would be rejoicing in hell at the very thought of it. But it cannot be. It is *forever*. They are cast into outer darkness.

Does God want anybody to go to hell?

Hell was never prepared for man. It is a place that was prepared by God for the devil and his angels, and the only reason that any man will go to hell will be because he follows the devil to hell.

Everybody in this world is the subject of either one of two masters. Either you belong to God or you belong to Satan. Either you have taken your stand for Jesus Christ

[1] Matt. xxii. 13.

or you have taken your stand against Him and on the side of Satan. Either you are a child of God or you are a child of the devil, and according to the Word of God you must go where your leader goes. If you are following the Lord Jesus Christ, your final resting place will be Heaven, but if you are following the devil, you must go with him to his final place of abode, which is hell. The Bible says that, "No man can serve two masters: for either he will hate the one, and love the other; or else he will hold to the one, and despise the other. Ye cannot serve God and mammon."[1]

Do not forget it; if you insist upon rejecting Jesus Christ, if you insist upon going on in your sin, you remain a child of Satan; you are on the devil's side; you are following in his train. Some day he is going to be cast into the hell that was prepared for him, and if you are one of his disciples, then of course *you* must go there too.

The Bible tells us, furthermore, that God is "not willing that any should perish, but that all should come to repentance. As I live, saith the Lord God, I have no pleasure in the death of the wicked; but that the wicked turn from his way and live: turn ye, turn ye from your evil ways; for why will ye die?"[2]

Salvation has been provided. There is a way to be saved from hell. Anybody that is wise, anyone who is sensible, will do everything within his power to flee from the wrath to come, and the way of escape has been provided: "For God so loved the world, that he gave his only begotten Son, that whosoever believeth in him should not perish, but have everlasting life. As many as received him, to them gave he power to become the sons of God, even to them that believe on his Name. The wages of sin is death; but the gift of God is eternal life through Jesus Christ our Lord."[3]

[1] Matt. vi. 24. [2] 2 Pet. iii. 9; Ezek. xxxiii. 11.
[3] Rom. vi. 23.

Life is available. You can make sure now of Heaven; you do not need to spend eternity in hell. There is a way of escape, but the Bible tells us that those who go to hell, those who spend eternity in hell, those who must some day go through the perpetual agony of an everlasting death, will do so only because they would not be saved.

"How often would I," exclaimed Jesus, "and ye would not."[1] And again, "Ye will not come to me, that ye might have life,"[2] or again, "I have called, and ye refused; I have stretched out my hand, and no man regarded."[3]

No wonder the Word of God says, "How shall we escape, if we neglect so great salvation?"[4] Whether you spend an eternity in Heaven—rejoicing, blessed, and saved, or whether you spend your eternity in the hopelessness of an everlasting death of body and soul in hell, is up to you. You *can* be saved, if you *will* be saved.

Now one last question and we are through. Listen to it carefully. You say, You have answered the question, "Why should there be a hell?" You have answered the question, "What is hell?" You have answered the question, "Does God want anybody to go to hell?" But now answer the final question if you can:

Where is hell?

There is only one answer to that question: hell—this place of everlasting destruction of soul and body, this place of misery and woe and despair, this eternal dwelling-place of the doomed and the damned, this place of hopelessness and eternal darkness, this place of everlasting separation from God, this place called hell—where is it? Hell is at the end of a Christless life.

[1] Matt. xxiii. 37.
[2] John v. 40.
[3] Prov. i. 24.
[4] Heb. ii. 3.

LOVE, COURTSHIP, AND THE CHRISTIAN HOME

FROM THE BIBLE

"Likewise, ye wives, be in subjection to your own husbands; that, if any obey not the word, they also may without the word be won by the conversation of the wives; While they behold your chaste conversation coupled with fear. Whose adorning let it not be that outward adorning of plaiting the hair, and of wearing of gold, or of putting on of apparel; But let it be the hidden man of the heart, in that which is not corruptible, even the ornament of a meek and quiet spirit, which is in the sight of God of great price. For after this manner in the old time the holy women also, who trusted in God, adorned themselves, being in subjection unto their own husbands: Even as Sara obeyed Abraham, calling him lord: whose daughters ye are, as long as ye do well, and are not afraid with any amazement. Likewise, ye husbands, dwell with them according to knowledge, giving honour unto the wife, as unto the weaker vessel, and as being heirs together of the grace of life; that your prayers be not hindered."[1]

[1] I Pet. iii. 1–7.

CHAPTER IV

LOVE, COURTSHIP, AND THE CHRISTIAN HOME

IT was a good sigh. It was the kind that indicates either great distress or complete contentment.

I had been standing beside one of the pillars that supported the boys' dormitory, watching the long double file of very, very happy boys and girls making their way from the dining hall to the girls' dormitory and the rather glum-looking single file of boys coming back from the girls' dormitory to ours. Some of the boys spoke to me; some did not. One or two stopped to chat for a few minutes. Then Lee came. The sigh escaped just as he came abreast of me. I was not quite sure what it meant.

"What's wrong, Lee? Are you ill?"

"No, I have never felt better in my life. As a matter of fact I am right on top of the world." His voice was strong but he had a dreamy far-away look in his eyes.

"According to the sigh you just heaved, I'd conclude that you were about to die. What else could cause such an eruption?"

"I'm in love."

"You're in love? And what does it feel like to be in love?"

I was quite young at the time and still fairly innocent. None of my close friends had ever actually fallen in love before, nor had I. I was excited to find someone with whom I was well acquainted that was in love. Now at last I could get some first-hand information about a very interesting subject.

57

By this time Lee and I had walked down the corridor and into my room. He was sitting down with that vacant expression on his face and he had not yet answered my question. I repeated it, "Well, tell me, what does it feel like?"

He looked more bewildered than ever. At last, after fiddling with his tie for a few seconds, he answered with a little hesitancy: "It's a sort of tickle around your heart that you can't scratch."

As I look back upon those days and think of Lee's answer today, I am forced to smile. However, in all probability he was as close to the truth as anyone has ever been. His definition of love was just about as valuable as any of the thousands that have been given by man. People have been trying to describe this, the greatest of human emotions, for as long as man has lived. The philosophers, the psychologists, the educators, the poets, the news commentators, the columnists, and even the preachers of our world have tried times without number to present an accurate definition or description of love to the world.

The only authoritative definition of love is to be found in the Bible. As a matter of fact, the Bible contains the answers to all of the major problems of life. The tragedy of the average Christian's experience is that he goes everywhere else first as he seeks the answers to his questions and comes to the Bible only as a last resort. Many a Christian young person looks for the answers from man and after he has made an irreparable mess of his life as a result of following the counsel of man, he makes his way to his pastor's study and his attention is turned to the only absolute source of information, the Word of God. Then he gets his answer, but unfortunately it is usually too late. The advice of man has only created more problems, greater burdens, and stronger temptation. His ship of life has foundered on the rocks of man's wisdom and he has been cast adrift on a sea that is too turbulent for him. If only he had gone to God first how different the story of his life might have been!

In just five verses of scripture God gives us the only authoritative definition of love: "Husbands, love your wives, even as Christ also loved the church, and gave himself for it; that he might sanctify and cleanse it with the washing of water by the word, that he might present it to himself a glorious church, not having spot, or wrinkle, or any such thing; but that it should be holy and without blemish. So ought men to love their wives as their own bodies. He that loveth his wife loveth himself. For no man ever yet hated his own flesh; but nourisheth and cherisheth it, even as the Lord the church."[1]

Here is God's answer to one of man's problems. The Bible says "husbands love your wives", and without doing violence to the Word of God we may conclude that the converse of this statement is equally true—"wives, love your husbands." This is a description of the kind of love that will result in a happy marriage and a Christian home that can expect the blessing of God to rest upon it.

God says two things in these verses. First, man is basically egotistical. Every man loves himself more than anyone else in the world. He thinks more of himself. He treats himself better. He makes allowances for his own mistakes. He bears with his own shortcomings. He sacrifices for his own pleasure or security. He provides for himself, nourishes himself, and protects himself more than anyone else in the world. Man loves himself.

Second, God makes it clear that if a man has the kind of love for someone else that can result in a happy marriage he must love the other person as he loves himself. This excludes selfishness. It means he will treat the other

[1] Eph. v. 25–29.

person as he would treat himself; plan for the other person as he would plan for himself; bear with the other's shortcomings as he bears with his own shortcomings; make allowances for the mistakes of the other person as he makes allowances for his own mistakes; care for, nourish, and think of the other person as he does himself. In short, he must love the other person as he loves himself. When this kind of love is in evidence, he can be assured that he has the potential of a happy marriage and a Christian home that can enjoy the blessings of God. Any other kind of affection carries with it no guarantee of a successful union.

Courtship

Here is a young Christian girl who comes to her pastor for advice: "I have been keeping company with a very fine young man. He has a good position. He comes from a lovely family, but he is not a Christian and has no interest in the things of God. Should I marry him?"

This situation and question could be multiplied a thousand times because it happens almost every day. I have been asked the same question by Christian young people dozens of times. When that question comes to me I always turn the attention of the person to the Word of God, where again she will find the only authoritative answer. No pastor or Christian worker in himself would dare to attempt an answer to such a personal and important question. But God gives us the answer and there is no doubt about it.

"Be ye not unequally yoked together with unbelievers: for what fellowship hath righteousness with unrighteousness? and what communion hath light with darkness? And what concord hath Christ with Belial? or what part hath he that believeth with an infidel? And what agreement hath the temple of God with idols? for ye are the temple of the living God; as God hath said, I will dwell in them, and walk in them; and I will be their God, and they shall be my people."[1]

This is God's answer and it cannot be questioned nor can there be any doubt whatsoever as to the interpretation.

God sets forth a very strong argument in these three vital verses. If an Old Testament Jew had wanted to do something that was particularly blasphemous, he might have secured an idol from one of the heathen tribes that surrounded Israel, carried it into the temple of God, set it up in front of the Holy of Holies, and worshipped his own God, Jehovah, and the graven image at the same time.

Such an action in the minds of Old Testament people would not only have been horribly blasphemous but practically impossible. It would have been inconceivable to even attempt the worship of Jehovah and the worship of an idol at the same time and in the same temple.

"Go ahead and do it, but it won't work." This would have been the reaction of any Jew in Old Testament days to such a preposterous proposal. The worship of Jehovah and the worship of idols do not mix and it is impossible for anyone to succeed in uniting them, because they are incompatible.

It is just as impossible for a Christian to unite his life with an unbeliever. Legally, it can be done, but practically it will not succeed, and wherever it is attempted there is no fellowship, no communion, no concord, no agreement. The result is always discord, strife, and marital chaos.

After these four verses have been pointed out to the average young person that is on the brink of a disastrous marriage, she will usually say as a last desperate resort, "But we're in love. I love him so much and he is so very

[1] 2 Cor. vi. 14-16.

fond of me that I believe in our case it will work out all right."

I believe that this should be shouted from the house-tops so loudly and so incessantly that every Christian young person could hear it: *the fact that you are in love does not make it right for you to break the law of God and the fact you are in love will not make it succeed when you do so*. God declares that the unequal yoke will not work, and you cannot make it work. This is not a suggestion; it is a command: "Be ye not unequally yoked together with unbelievers."[1]

The Christian home

The objective of love and courtship for the Christian young person, of course, is the establishment of a Christian home and the rearing of a Christian family.

Houses that are made out of bricks and mortar normally have four walls. A building that did not have four walls could scarcely be called a house. There are four walls in the Christian home. If these are erected in your home you have a Christian home, but if any of these walls are missing, you do not have a Christian home, even though everyone in your family is a Christian.

Discipline

The wall of *discipline* must be erected in every Christian home. There are two basic philosophies of life in our world. All of the philosophical systems of man can be divided into these two classes. There is the philosophy of the world and the devil and there is the philosophy of the Bible and Jesus.

The philosophy of this world can be summarized in four words: "Do as you please!" Most of the people in our generation have built their lives around this philosophy of

[1] 2 Cor. vi. 14.

self-expression. Live your own life, fulfil your own ambitions, try to realize your own desires and aspirations, and do everything within your power to make your own dreams come true. Go where you want to go, do what you want to do, think as you want to think and, in general, live your own life. "Do as you please!" Our world is rapidly going to hell on the band waggon of this satanic philosophy.

The philosophy of the Bible and Jesus is "Discipline." Discipline is essential in every Christian home and God's Word makes it clear that it involves everyone in the family from the youngest to the oldest—the children, the adolescents, and the adults.

No matter how clever Christian parents may think their children are, the Bible declares that if they are left to make their own decisions they will act foolishly. "Foolishness is bound in the heart of a child; but the rod of correction shall drive it far from him."[1] Leave a child to express himself and he will make mistakes, simply because his little mind is not sufficiently developed to make the right decisions. Therefore there must be "the rod of correction" which will steer him in the right direction when he would go the wrong way. The "rod of correction" does not necessarily refer to corporal punishment but to disciplinary measures of any kind. There are many different varieties of rods but the end product is always the same—discipline.

Most adult Christians are willing to admit this point as far as children are concerned, because it does not affect them personally. However, the Bible teaches that discipline—"the rod of correction"—does not end with childhood but is an essential characteristic of our entire Christian lives. The Christian is a man whose life is governed by discipline.

[1] Prov. xxii. 15.

Many times the Word of God refers to the Christian as a soldier. "Put on the whole armour of God."[1] Hymnology is filled with songs about Christian soldiers—"Sound the Battle Cry," "Onward Christian Soldiers," "Hold the Fort," etc. The Christian then is a soldier.

Is there any sphere of life in which discipline is more essential than the military? The armies of this world function and win their battles with discipline. When there is an enemy to be routed from his position the captain does not ask his men if they would like to attack, he simply issues a command: "Charge!" and the soldiers obey his orders. Without discipline no army could operate and no battles would be won.

The Christian is in the army of the Lord. Jesus Christ is the Captain of his salvation. He is not living for himself. He is not trying to fulfil his own ambitions and desires. He is marching under the command of a higher power. He does not express himself, he obeys the commands of God. His life is disciplined by the precepts of the Word of God. Therefore, if any home is to be called Christian, the wall of *discipline* must be erected.

Good example

The second wall that must be built in every home if it is to be called Christian is the wall of *good example*. Modern psychologists tell us that most of what we know we learn from watching "models." A "model" is any person whom we use as an example. The people we imitate are our "models" because we model our lives after the pattern of theirs. As we grow older of course our "models" become numerous, complex, and usually composite. When a child is very young his "models" are quite simple.

[1] Eph. vi. 11.

In the majority of cases, from the time he is born until he is five or six years of age, the only "models" a child has are his mother and father. He does not see others often enough to imitate them. Most of what a child learns during these formative years does not come from the instruction of his parents but from their lives as they live before him. He does not try to do what they tell him to do; he attempts to do what they do.

The average baby smiles when you look at him in his crib. Why is it that he does not frown or stick out his tongue at you? Simply because every time his mother brings that bottle of milk to her baby, as she puts it in his mouth, she smiles. Gradually the baby associates the satisfaction he gets from the bottle with the expression he sees on his mother's face, and he tries to imitate her. His first few attempts may turn out to be a scowl rather than a smile, but finally he learns how to control the tiny muscles of his face and he reproduces what he sees in his mother. He has learned to smile because he has seen her smile.

Why do babies go through the trouble of learning to walk? It is an extremely difficult procedure for a little bow-legged baby who is actually too heavy for his legs to try to walk. It is much easier for him to crawl. Nobody has to teach a child to crawl. As soon as his muscles are strong enough to lift his body off the floor he is able to crawl quite successfully. It seems to come naturally, but walking on two legs is an entirely different matter. Why does the baby put forth such an effort to walk? Simply because his mother and his father walk. Every time he sees them they are standing upright. When they go past him they walk. When they bring him something they walk. When they carry him they walk, and he wants to do what they do.

Every individual in this world is a product, not only of

E

his heredity, but also of his environment, and in the normal home environment for the first five or six years consists of the example of a mother and a father. That is why in the Christian home good example is so important. To a large extent your child will be in later life what you are now. That is why English children have an English accent, Scottish children have a Scottish accent, and Southern children have a Southern accent. That is why French children speak French, Spanish children speak Spanish and Russian children speak Russian. They have learned from listening to their mother and father and attempting to imitate them.

People who use good grammar usually did not learn it in school but at home, because their mothers and fathers spoke correctly. I have met a great many who have had a complete high-school education and sometimes even a few years in university, but who do not speak correctly—not because they did not know the rules of grammar, but because they came from homes where their parents spoke poorly, and they are a product of the homes from which they came.

Show me a father that is living in sin with no interest in God, and in nine cases out of ten I will show you a son that is going in exactly the same direction. Show me a father who is a godly man, and in the majority of cases I will show you a son who is following in his father's footsteps. Show me a girl who swears and uses profane language, and usually I can trace her back to a mother who did exactly the same thing, but show me a girl who is living a good moral life, and in almost every case I can trace her back to a godly mother.

That is why the Bible says, "Train up a child in the way he should go: and when he is old, he will not depart from it."[1] What a child is when he becomes old is the

[1] Prov. xxii. 6.

result, to a large extent, of what his parents were when he was young. The wall of *good example* is an intrinsic part of the Christian home.

Family worship

No family can call itself Christian in the strict sense of the word until they have erected in their home the wall of *family worship*—that time when the entire family gathers around the Word of God and is united before the throne of God. This is family worship and it is essential to a Christian home.

Any amount of attendance at church services or evangelistic campaigns, or faithfulness to the mid-week prayer meeting, or study of the Word of God in the Bible class, can never take the place of family worship. The Roman Catholic Church one time attempted to emphasize the necessity of family worship with the motto, "The family that prays together stays together." This is excellent advice. There is no factor that will do more to bind a family into a harmonious unity than the family altar. Not only does the Bible solve the problems of a man's personal life, but it also solves the problems of his family life. It will go a long way toward settling family quarrels and eliminating family differences. Discord and strife do not mix well with the Word of God and prayer.

Despite the necessity of the family altar in every Christian home, it is shocking to know how many Christian families there are that have never established the family altar in their homes. They never read the Bible as a family and they never pray as a family. Then they wonder why it is that the blessing of God does not rest in its abundance upon their home. No home can call itself Christian that does not have a family altar. This wall must be erected.

Salvation

Finally, the wall of *salvation* must be built. This wall is basic and no home can ever be truly Christian until the wall of salvation has been erected—until every member of the family is a Christian.

The other three walls—discipline, good example, and family worship—could conceivably be built in a home that was not Christian at all, but the building of these walls would not make a home Christian. The wall of *salvation* is the basic factor in any Christian home. After it has been built, these other walls should follow, but as long as one member of the family has not been saved, that family is not really a Christian family and will not enjoy the full blessing of God that is the privilege of the truly Christian home.

When a person becomes a child of God, their first responsibility is to their own family and God expects them to do everything within their power to win their loved ones to the Lord Jesus Christ. That is why the Apostle Paul answered the Philippian jailer's question by saying, "Believe on the Lord Jesus Christ, and thou shalt be saved, and thy house."[1] Paul was urging him to accept Christ as his own personal Saviour and to do everything within his power to win his family to Christ as well.

The salvation of the unsaved members of the family is dependent upon two things. First, the faith, testimony, and prayer of those members of the family that are already Christians. Second, the decision of the unsaved members of the family to trust Christ as their own personal Saviour in response to the testimony of those that are saved. These are the ingredients of salvation in any situation on the human level. Someone must tell the story and testify to

[1] Acts xvi. 31.

its truth, and someone must accept the testimony and respond to the invitation.

In some cases, the reason the family is not wholly Christian is that the testimony of those who are Christians has been weak, and has not been supported by a real Christian life. In other cases, the testimony has been good and beyond any criticism whatsoever, but the unsaved members of the family have simply refused to yield for one reason or another.

I know some fathers who are the only members of their families that have not accepted Christ. Their children and their wives have testified to them again and again and prayed for them incessantly, but these fathers have been too stubborn and too fond of their own sin to turn from it and turn to God. As a result, they have prevented the family whom they claim to love from enjoying the full blessing of God.

I have met some mothers who have refused to yield to the Lord Jesus Christ despite the fact that their entire families have urged them to do so again and again, but they are too self-willed and self-centred. They have gone in their own way with their backs turned toward God, and consequently, their families have not enjoyed the blessing of God upon their homes.

What a tragedy that fathers and mothers and sisters and brothers, who profess that they love one another, should not be willing to forget themselves long enough to get right with God and complete the Christian family circle by building the wall of salvation!

If your home is truly Christian, the walls of *discipline*, *good example*, *family worship*, and *salvation* must be built. Are they built in your home? If so, you have a Christian home. If not, you do not have a Christian home.

CHAPTER V

THE INTELLIGENT FOOL

FROM THE BIBLE

"And one of the company said unto him, Master, speak to my brother, that he divide the inheritance with me. And he said unto him, Man, who made me a judge or a divider over you? And he said unto them, Take heed, and beware of covetousness: for a man's life consisteth not in the abundance of the things which he possesseth, And he spake a parable unto them, saying, The ground of a certain rich man brought forth plentifully: And he thought within himself, saying, What shall I do, because I have no room where to bestow my fruits? And he said, This will I do: I will pull down my barns, and build greater; and there will I bestow all my fruits and my goods. And I will say to my soul, Soul, thou hast much goods laid up for many years; take thine ease, eat, drink, and be merry. But God said unto him, Thou fool, this night thy soul shall be required of thee: then whose shall those things be, which thou hast provided? So is he that layeth up treasure for himself, and is not rich toward God."[1]

[1] Luke xii. 13–21.

CHAPTER V

THE INTELLIGENT FOOL

THE crop was good. Almost too good. The barns were full and there was grain standing in the fields and fruit in the orchards. Obviously, the harvest had to be gathered and stored. The farmer decided to tear down his old barns and build greater.

He was in the midst of his plans for the future when God spoke to him, and called him a fool. "Thou fool, this night thy soul shall be required of thee: then whose shall those things be, which thou hast provided?"[1]

When God calls a man a fool there must be something seriously wrong with him. The word "fool" in the eyes of God is a terrible word with which to accuse a man. So terrible is it, that Jesus once warned His disciples that if any man called his brother a fool he would be in danger of hell-fire.

It is wise, then, that we look closely into the character and the deeds of this man whom God called a fool and discover why God accused him.

In many ways he was commendable. Certainly God did not call him a fool because of his good qualities.

Wealthy

He was a wealthy man. God did not call him a fool for being wealthy. Jesus said that it is hard for a rich man to enter into the Kingdom of Heaven, but He did not say

[1] Luke xii. 20.

that it is impossible. God does not frown on wealth that has been earned honestly, if it is used in the proper manner and allocated to its proper place in our thinking.

It is only when the *almighty dollar* takes the place of Almighty God that it becomes an obstacle to the Kingdom of God. God does not attach any particular stigma to the state of wealth. It is almost as easy for poverty to keep a man out of Heaven as it is for wealth to do so. I know some people who make a God out of their poverty.

This man was wealthy, but that is not why God called him a fool.

Industrious

He was an industrious man. Land does not produce a large crop unless someone has toiled by the sweat of his brow to plough it and cultivate it, to weed it and work it in such a way that the soil, the sun, and the rain have every opportunity of producing the crop.

At this point the Bible gives us concrete reason to believe that Jesus was talking, not about some lazy, careless individual who refused to work, but rather about a very industrious, hard-working man. That assuredly was a very commendable feature of his character.

Intelligent

He was a thinking man: "And he thought within himself."[1] Here was a real problem with which he had to deal—a big crop and insufficient room in the barns. He looked at his crop. He noticed the size of his barns, and then he sat down to think, and to decide how he might solve this important problem. God found no fault with him because he stopped to think.

[1] Luke xii. 17.

God has given us a head and a portion of brains, and He intends us to use them. We need more Christian people that are willing and ready, and not too lazy, to think. We have a certain amount of equipment with which to deal with life as we meet it from day to day, and God will not do for us what He has given us the power to do for ourselves.

Some Christians think of God as a sort of handyman who will solve all their problems for them, clothe them and feed them, tell them what to say and when to say it, and, in general, leave them to "be carried to the skies on flowery beds of ease, while others fight to win the prize, and sail through bloody seas."

I am reminded of the hypothetical character who was stopped by a policeman at one of the busy intersections of a large city. He had set out to cross the road with his eyes shut. Upon being questioned as to his reasons for doing such a foolish thing, he answered that the Lord, who cares for the lilies of the field and sees the sparrow that falls to the ground, would see that he was not struck by a car. He seemed to have forgotten that God had given him a pair of eyes with which to see his way across the street.

True, God supplies the food, but we must feed ourselves. God has supplied the eyes and ears, the nose and mouth, the arms and legs, along with all the rational powers that we have, but it is our job to see that they are used as they should be. The adage is old, but I believe true, "The Lord helps those who help themselves," and, we might add, those who are unable to help themselves. The glory of being a Christian is not that we may have our work done for us, but that when we can do no more, and yet all has not been done, we can call on a never-failing source of supply and expect God to do the thing that to man seems impossible.

Here was a thinking man, and for this God did not condemn him.

Ambitious

He was an ambitious man. He wanted to get ahead in the world. He was anxious to make something of himself. He was eager to succeed. This, too, is a commendable element in the man's character. God did not call him a fool for being ambitious.

Some people seem to have the idea that the ultimate in Christian living is to be a failure. Their theme song seems to be, "Oh, to be nothing!" The Christian should not worry about getting ahead in life. He should not strive to succeed. He should not care about bettering his condition. He should be devoid of any ambition.

If God can be disgusted at all, He must be thoroughly disgusted with such an attitude as this. Furthermore, if God has called a man to do a certain job, no matter what sphere of life he may be in, he should be able to do it better than the man who is not a Christian.

And why not? Why should the Christian have no ambition? Why should he not succeed? The ordinary person goes into his profession or business alone. But we are the sons of God. We are joint heirs with Jesus Christ, and when a Christian does anything, he does it— not alone—but backed by the almighty power of God.

Why be a failure when you can demonstrate the power of God in your life by your success? Why be content to remain in the ditch throwing the dirt up, when by the grace of God you could be foreman of the job? There is nothing wrong with the man who does the digging. God never frowns on hard or dirty work, but there is something wrong with the man who digs without keeping his eyes on the top of the ditch and endeavouring to get up there eventually.

God does not delight in failures. We need more Christians who are leaders in our country. We need Christian reeves and Christian mayors. We need Christian store-keepers and Christian policemen—men and women who are industrious—men and women who are leaders—men and women who are topping their class.

The most successful man in any town or city should be the Christian. He has all the power of God to help him.

No, God never condemns ambition as long as it is turned in the right direction, and the glory is given to Him. He did not call this man a fool because he was ambitious.

Respectable

This man was a respectable citizen. He had a good reputation in his community. The man who lives riotously and immorally, the man who does not work hard, the man who lives by night and sleeps by day, will not be as successful as this farmer. Good crops and fast living do not mix. Progress and strong drink do not go together. Success does not come with riotous living.

This farmer must certainly have been respectable. He was the kind of man the local lodges and societies would like to have had as one of their members. He was a man who would add prestige to any organization. Everyone probably admired him and thought well of him. His signature would give a man a position. He was a good man, an upright man, a moral man, an honest man. And yet, as we read the narrative, we find, to our amazement, that God called him a fool.

. . . . .

In the eyes of God this man was a fool for three reasons.

He neglected his soul

He spoke to his soul and said, "Take thine ease, eat, drink, and be merry."[1] These are things that should have been said to his body, for only the body with its capacity for sensation can take ease, eat, drink, and be merry. But for this man, soul and body were one and the same thing. He thought that the body constitutes the man. He did not consider the fact that there was a part of himself—the real man—which he had neglected, a part that could not be fed and satisfied with the things that satisfy the body.

In modern language, he would be called a mechanistic materialist—one who thinks the only existence is that which is substantial, concrete material, things that he can grasp, things that he can see and feel and hear. Man, to the materialist, is a mere collection of chemical properties that react in certain ways under certain conditions. He is a bundle of nerves and sensations, a complex organism of stimuli and reflexes, a sort of machine that can be satisfied by food and drink and rest.

He was like the biologist who denies the existence of the soul merely because he cannot find it when he dissects the human body. As though everything that has a real existence can be found! Can we dissect the rose and find its beauty? Certainly not, but who will deny that the rose is beautiful? Can we dissect the man and find love? Certainly not, but do we deny the existence of love? Can we take the laugh of a child as it plays on the street, put it into a test tube, analyse it, and extract the joy? Certainly not, but the joy is there.

It is the things which are not material that make the world worthwhile—the joy in the heart of a child, the love of a mother, the protection of a father, the beauty of a rose,

[1] Luke xii. 19.

the happiness in the wag of a dog's tail, the contentment in the "moo" of a cow, the satisfaction in the purr of a kitten, the harmony in the colours of a rainbow, and the glory in the crimson of a sunset. These are the things that are intangible, the things that we cannot dissect, the things we cannot find; but these are the things that are real, the things that are valuable.

There are thousands of people who think of the world and of themselves as did this man. They forget that when God created man He breathed into the material of his body the breath of life, and that he became a living soul— a soul that lives forever, an eternal personality. In forgetting this, they forget to prepare for the needs of the soul, not knowing that the provisions they have made for the body must some day be left behind, that some day they must "shuffle off this mortal coil" and stand as living souls before God, unprepared.

God thinks of the materialist as a "fool," and the day is coming when He will call him by his own name.

He neglected God

He thought that everything he had was his own. Notice the preponderance of personal pronouns in his words: "And *he* thought within *himself*, saying, What shall *I* do, because *I* have no room where to bestow *my* fruits? And *he* said, This will *I* do: *I* will pull down *my* barns, and build greater; and there will *I* bestow all *my* fruits and *my* goods. And *I* will say to *my* soul, Soul, thou hast much goods laid up for many years"[1]—*I*, *my* fruits, *my* barns, *my* goods, *my* soul, etc.

In the Old Testament a reference is made to another man who was confronted with very much the same kind of problem as was this man. He, too, had reaped a great

[1] Luke xii. 17–19.

harvest, and he had stopped to consider what he should do with it. But notice the decision he makes. Self is entirely forgotten, and God is glorified; for he says, "What shall I render unto the Lord for all his benefits toward me?"[1] What a difference! In the one case the man makes plans for himself but neglects God entirely. In the other case the man forgets himself entirely, but remembers God.

What about you? God has blessed you. Have you remembered Him? If you have not, then just as surely as God called this man a fool, He will call you a fool, because you have neglected Him.

He neglected eternity

Here was a man who was concerned about the future, but his future was measured only in terms of time. "Thou hast much goods laid up for many years."[2] From the endless extension of eternity he had segregated a few short years. All of his energy and brain power had been concentrated upon preparing for these years, and eternity had been entirely neglected.

His greatest concern was to be happy while he lived upon earth. But the happiness for which he longed was always in the future. Before he could become happy, he had to realize a great building programme. He would have had to spend years laying in a store of goods and in building up his wealth, and then—away off somewhere in the hypothetical future—he would take his ease, eat, drink, and be merry.

But he never achieved happiness. That is always the experience of the man outside of Jesus Christ. Happiness is forever in the future. He strives for it, but never realizes it. He reaches for it, but never grasps it. It

[1] Ps. cxvi. 12.   [2] Luke xii. 19.

evades him at every turning. His ship never comes in. He looks forward to the years of his retirement, when he thinks he can settle down and spend his wealth—only to find that when those years come he is too old to enjoy them.

How different is the experience of the Christian! For him, happiness is always in the present. Joy begins the moment he accepts Christ as his Saviour, and that joy continues throughout eternity. "Whoso trusteth in the Lord, happy is he."[1]

This rich farmer neglected eternity, and lost for both time and eternity. Somewhere out in the great beyond he lives. But he lives the life of a lost soul. He is separated from God. He is separated from everything that is good and from all that makes for happiness. He is in hell—not because of his great sin, but because he planned only for his natural life, and failed to prepare for his eternal life. God called him a fool, because he neglected eternity.

If you, like him, are spending all your time and energy in preparation for this present life, and in doing so you have neglected eternity, God looks upon you as a fool.

This man was commendable for many reasons, but he was a fool. You, too, may be wealthy. You may be industrious. You may have great ambitions and lofty aspirations. You may be moral, above-board, and held high in esteem by your friends and neighbours, but if you have neglected your *soul*, your *God*, and your *eternity*, regardless of your attributes, God calls you a fool. Some day He will complete the indictment, "This night thy soul shall be required of thee: then whose shall those things be, which thou hast provided?"[2]

[1] Prov. xvi. 20.   [2] Luke xii. 13–21.

F

CHAPTER VI

THE SCARLET SIN

"And it came to pass, after the year was expired, at the time when kings go forth to battle, that David sent Joab, and his servants with him, and all Israel, and they destroyed the children of Ammon, and besieged Rabbah. But David tarried still at Jerusalem. And it came to pass in an evening-tide, that David arose from off his bed, and walked upon the roof of the king's house: and from the roof he saw a woman washing herself; and the woman was very beautiful to look upon. And David sent and inquired after the woman. And one said, Is not this Bathsheba, the daughter of Eliam, the wife of Uriah the Hittite? And David sent messengers, and took her; and she came in unto him, and he lay with her; for she was purified from her uncleanness: and she returned unto her house. And the woman conceived, and sent and told David, and said, I am with child. And it came to pass in the morning, that David wrote a letter to Joab, and sent it by the hand of Uriah. And he wrote in the letter, saying, Set ye Uriah in the forefront of the hottest battle, and retire ye from him, that he may be smitten, and die."[1]

[1] 2 Sam. xi. 1–5, 14–15.

CHAPTER VI

THE SCARLET SIN

THIS is the story of what sin can do to either a saint or a sinner. For that reason it is important that every man and woman and boy and girl pay close attention. No matter who you are, no matter what your circumstances in life, no matter what your spiritual standing may be, this is the story of what could happen to you.

From this account I want to point out three things. First, I would like to describe the character of the man who sinned. Second, I want to say something about why David was such an easy prey to temptation. Finally, I must take time to trace the course and the results of David's sin.

The man who sinned

The Bible is filled with references to David. Let me indicate three factors about this man who committed adultery and murder. Unlike other men mentioned in the Word of God, he was a man after God's own heart. Even before Samuel anointed him to be King of Israel, as the veteran prophet spoke about the young man he said, "The Lord hath sought him a man after his own heart."[1]

David began the line of kings through which Jesus came into the world. Joseph, whose wife was the mother of Jesus, was a direct descendant of King David, and David not only began that line of kings but he established

[1] I Sam. xiii. 14.

the throne upon which Jesus will some day sit and rule the world during the Millennium: "The Lord God shall give unto him the throne of his father David."[1]

David was one of the inspired writers—as a matter of fact, one of the greatest. He wrote many of the psalms that we read again and again for comfort and inspiration and exhortation and blessing.

It is hard to believe that the Spirit-inspired poet who penned the lines of the twenty-third Psalm was the Satan-inspired perpetrator of a crime so bestial, brutal, and barbaric that the average comparatively decent individual is caused to blush as he reads the account.

David then, the man around whom this tragic story centres, was not an ordinary man; he was not a man who had had no opportunity, but rather he was a mountain-peak among Bible characters. When we realize that David—this man who fell into one of the most loathsome sins that it is possible for man to commit—was God's Goliath of the Old Testament, it behooves even the most devoted saint, as well as the most debauched sinner, to sit up and pay attention, for once again let me repeat: *the story of David could well be the story of you or of me, no matter who we are.*

Let the moral guard of the most stalwart of modern spiritual giants be lowered but for a moment and he becomes an easy target for the flat smooth stone from the sling shot of Satan's stripling.

Notice the tremendous depth to which David fell. David's was a fall from the greatness of a spiritual Leviathan to the gutter of adultery and murder. It was the descent of a man from the dominion of a king to the depravity of a criminal. It was the retrogression of a heart from the purity of piety to the impurity of passion. What an awful fall!

[1] Luke i. 32.

Why David sinned

Let me say four things about why David was such an easy prey to temptation. First, as I read the account, I notice that *David was an easy prey for temptation because he was inactive.*

This was that time of year, the Bible tells us, "when kings go forth to battle."[1] David had sent Joab and his servants and all Israel out to fight, but we are told that David "tarried still in Jerusalem."[1] Obviously, this was not his custom. David had always been a man of war. David had always been in the forefront of the battle. David's life had always been filled with activity and work and fighting, but at this particular time, for some strange reason, although Joab went forth and the valiant men of war went forth and all the rest who were able went forth to battle, David stayed at home in Jerusalem.

With all the others away, being alone in Jerusalem, David found himself with spare time on his hands, and I believe one of the great contributing factors to his sin was that he was idle—he had nothing to do, he was on a vacation, he had too much free time.

I do not know of any time when temptation is more likely to make an attack against our lives than when we allow ourselves to be inactive. Sin is seldom conceived during working hours, in the midst of the stress and strain of business life. Sin is usually born in idle time.

It is not during the fighting that soldiers get into trouble, but during their leaves. It is on those week-ends and fortnights, when they are away from the actual firing line, that the men in the army get into the deepest sin.

Our boys and girls do not get involved with sinful companions and pleasures during their school hours, but during their free time after school and at night. It is in

[1] 2 Sam. xi. 1.

those hours of leisure, when they are out loitering with "the gang" on the street corner, that they undergo their most severe temptations. A great many modern parents contribute tremendously to the juvenile delinquency of their own children simply because they allow them to have too much liberty during their spare time. In our love and affection for our own children we often fail to give them the responsibility that is essential if they are to be kept from temptation and sin.

Sad to say, we are living in an age when the cry of the world—the cry of the working man and the cry of the working woman—for years now has been for shorter hours, less work, longer vacations, and an earlier period of retirement. Although all of these have their advantages, sometimes I wonder if the modern world, instead of pleading and struggling for something that is going to improve its lot, is not in a very real sense demanding more time to sin. It is idle hands that practise evil and idle minds that conceive sin. One of the most dangerous things that any man or any woman can do is to allow himself to have too much spare time, too much time in which to let his thoughts wander without discipline.

If the story of the scarlet sin of David and Bathsheba does nothing else, it does cry out to us with a warning note, whether we are sinners or saints: "Beware, beware of too much leisure time. It seems desirable but it is devastating; it appears delightful but it is destructive; it beckons toward satisfaction but it breeds sorrow; it looks tempting but it leads into temptation."

David was an easy prey for temptation because he was exempt from authority and beyond responsibility. David, you will remember, was a king, and although it was a responsible position, yet he himself was beyond the authority of other people. He made the laws in a very real sense in his day and, I suppose, concluded that no one could force him to keep his own laws. David was in the unfortunate position of being morally accountable to no one but himself. He was beyond discipline, and I believe that one of the contributing factors to his sin was that he was not living a disciplined life.

When men and women are living a life of discipline they are much less likely to yield to temptation than when they lack it. In almost every aspect of modern life, discipline is lacking, and this deficiency, I believe, is one of the great contributing factors to the sin of our day.

In the majority of cases we lack discipline in our homes. Most fathers and mothers, fearing lest they should overdo it, fail to stress it enough, leaving their children deprived of one of the essentials of purity and righteousness. It is far better to have too much discipline than not enough. Weak discipline produces wayward young people. Unruled boys and girls, incubated in a "do-as-you-please" atmosphere, develop into riotous men and women.

We lack discipline in our schools. There are two ways to govern a school—by discipline and by honour. If you will look up the records of both, you will find that in the majority of cases the girls whose lives have been ruined and the young people who have become entangled in sin while they were at school, have lived in one that was based on the honour system. On the other hand, the schools that usually have an absolutely clean record are almost inevitably disciplinarian institutions.

It is high time Christians realized that it is wrong—yes, it is unscriptural—to put our young people on the honour system. Human beings need discipline. The Bible is filled with it. The Word of God endorses it. Jesus teaches it, and where we fail to impose it we fail to be Christian to that extent and we leave our young people open to every kind of temptation.

Not only is there a lamentable lack in our homes and in our schools, but there is a deplorable deficiency of discipline in the lives of adult Christian individuals in our modern world today. Oh, how we need to learn that even as mature men and women we must discipline our lives. We need to surround ourselves by a wall of discipline that will protect us from the temptations of the world.

When the Bible says, "Flee also youthful lusts,"[1] it means not only to turn from things that are evil, but as far as possible to build such a bulwark of discipline around about us that it is impossible for us to sin. In other words, if you would resist temptation and avoid sin, I believe it is absolutely necessary that you put yourself in a position where it is difficult for you to sin. You cannot wander through an orchard of beehives without eventually getting stung. You cannot play with fire without some day getting burned, and you cannot expose yourself to temptation continually without sometime, somewhere along the line, yielding to that temptation.

In a great many cases you will discover that when people yield to sin they do so because, for some reason, they have been put into a position where the normal discipline and restrictions of their lives have been removed so that it has become easy for them to fall into temptation.

Almost every man who served in the last great world war, or as a matter of fact in any war, can cite case after case such as this: A young man who has lived a regulated and disciplined and normal life at home joined the army, the air force, or the navy. Before long he found himself doing things that he would never have dreamed of doing at home—associating with people with whom he would never have associated at home—yielding to temptations that would have appalled him when he was at home.

[1] 2 Tim. ii. 22.

Why? Simply because whether a man be a soldier, a salesman, a business man, a preacher, or any other kind of person, when he gets away from the discipline of his home environment, when he is removed from those people and conventions and circumstances that have kept him on the straight and narrow way, he has to be a tremendously strong person to resist temptation. Sad to say, by far the majority are not strong enough.

When soldiers go away from home they live in cities where nobody knows them, they are in a situation where nobody cares about them, and they find themselves in a position where it does not matter what they do from a moral standpoint. Unfortunately, in a great percentage of instances, although the same men lived normally at home, although they had a disciplined life at home, although they were comparatively decent individuals at home, when they got away from the bonds of discipline of their home, they fell into sin.

David sinned because he was in a position where he was beyond the reach of discipline. I cannot urge you too strongly—if you would be saved from the smudge of sin, if you would be freed from the fear of falling, if you would be untroubled in the trial of temptation—put yourself as often as possible into circumstances in life where it is difficult for you to sin. You will have enough trouble with temptation even in a well-regulated life. How much more dangerous it is to remove the regulations, to remove the discipline, and to be compromised by a position where it is easy to sin.

David was an easy prey for temptation because he allowed himself to toy with temptation. It is dangerous to play with sin.

When David went out on the roof-top that first night I do not believe that he had any idea of adultery in his mind. He had no conception of murder, but he stood there and allowed himself to enjoy a little mild sinful pleasure. I suppose he reasoned: "That woman is in her own court-yard and I am here. This is my palace; this is my roof-top; it is not my fault if this evil passes before my eyes. I have no control over what I happen by accident to see. Therefore, there is no harm in staying here."

Of course, up to a point, David was right. I do not believe we are held responsible for the evil that by chance passes before our eyes and presents itself to our minds. When David saw Bathsheba for the first time bathing in her own courtyard he was absolutely passive as far as sin was concerned. David made his mistake when he returned to the roof-top the next night, as undoubtedly he did. Then he began actively to meditate and to ponder upon the possibility of sin.

He was not responsible as long as the sin passed before him by mere chance, but he became responsible the moment he deliberately put himself in a position where he could enjoy the sin of the world that was passing before him. Then he became an active agent as he began to meditate upon it and ponder over it and enjoy it.

Jesus said, "Whosoever looketh on a woman to lust after her hath committed adultery with her already in his heart."[1] Obviously, this does not mean that a man is responsible for every thought that passes through his mind and every sight that passes before his eyes. I do not know where I would be today if I were held responsible for every thought that by chance ever passed through my mind. If you will be honest with yourself and honest with God, you must admit that only God knows where you might be today if you had been held accountable for every thought that has ever happened to find its way through your mind and every sinful sight that by chance has passed before your eyes.

[1] Matt. v. 28.

Jesus was not referring here to what happened to David when he first saw Bathsheba and the thought first came to him that he might commit adultery with her. He was speaking about that second night after David had deliberately harboured that thought within his mind and had begun to ponder over the possibility of committing adultery. Then, as far as the Word of God is concerned, David had already committed adultery with Bathsheba in his heart.

The mere thought of sin is not wrong but harbouring a sin in the mind is just as bad as committing it. That is why the Psalmist said, "If I regard iniquity in my heart, the Lord will not hear me."[1] Thoughts inevitably result in action.

On that first night, if David had turned from the sight of Bathsheba and from the thought of adultery, if he had gone out immediately to join the others in the battle, if he had exerted his energy in another direction and put the thought of adultery out of his mind, I do not believe God would ever have had to punish him. But he did not do that. Not only did he see Bathsheba—not only did the thought of adultery present itself to his mind—but David toyed with sin; David played with the evil thought, and no one can harbour either a good thought or an evil thought for very long without eventually trying to put that thought into action.

David was an easy prey for temptation because he ignored his own weakness. After his sin with Bathsheba and his murder of Uriah, he recognized the basic weakness of his own nature and the fundamental frailty of the life of any man or any woman—that within him there was a natural tendency to sin over which he had to battle continually every day of his life. That is why in David's immortal psalm of confession he said, "I was shapen in iniquity; and in sin did my mother conceive me."[2]

[1] Ps. lxvi. 18.   [2] Ps. li. 5.

Apparently David had not guarded himself sufficiently against his own natural weakness, his own human bent to sinning. He had probably failed in his prayer life. He had neglected his communion with God. He had lost that contact with God that gave him power over his own intrinsic tendency toward sin.

The Apostle Paul knew that even as a Christian he had to battle continually against the old nature that wanted to sin. Paul realized that the Christian has two natures; he has one nature that is born of God as a result of trusting the Lord Jesus Christ as Saviour—a nature that hates sin, that is repulsed by sin—but he was aware of the fact that along with that new nature there was still some of the old human fleshly nature within him.

The entire seventh chapter of the Book of Romans portrays the struggle in his own life, and the struggle that goes on within the life of every Christian person between the two natures. Paul discovered that the only victory over the old nature lay in complete and continual yieldedness to the indwelling Christ. That is why he said, "In all these things we are more than conquerors through him that loved us."[1] Conquerors over what? Conquerors over the old nature that has a tendency to sin. How? Through Him that loved us.

This yieldedness to the Spirit of God, about which Paul spoke, is maintained only through a continual communion with God through the Lord Jesus Christ. When we lose contact with God, we are opening the door to the enemy that is within, and very soon the walls of our resistance are broken down completely.

It is not sufficient that you discipline your life. It is not sufficient that you limit your free time. It is not sufficient that you refuse to toy with sin. It is absolutely necessary that you keep continually in touch with the Power that

[1] Rom. viii. 37.

can defeat the tendency to sin that is within you. That is the danger to which Jesus was referring when He turned to Peter one day and said, "Watch and pray, that ye enter not into temptation: the spirit indeed is willing, but the flesh is weak."[1] David did not take account of man's intrinsic weakness—that tendency of the old nature to sin—and he became an easy prey for temptation.

Sin's path and penalty

Sin usually commences with an incident that is apparently harmless but inevitably terminates with consequences that are appallingly destructive.

David's sin started with a casual and apparently harmless glance at a naked woman, but it ended with adultery and murder and its consequences. That is the way sin always starts. Very few people plunge into vile sin all at one time on the impulse of a moment. Great sin is usually the culmination of a series of lesser sins. Sin starts small and ends big. It is hatched in insignificance and obscurity and breaks forth into prominence and publicity. It is born of a minor cause and develops into a major effect. It originates with a little carelessness and terminates in a tremendous catastrophe.

When I was in the island of Jamaica, one afternoon as we were riding on horseback through the hills, the missionary who was with me called my attention to a certain tree. It was tremendous—as large as any that I have ever seen, even in the forests of British Columbia. It had grown very, very tall and had a great many sturdy branches. When I first looked at the tree it seemed to be green and alive and flourishing, but then upon closer examination I noticed that it was absolutely dead. There was not a leaf on it, but

[1] Matt. xxvi. 41.

wound all around the tree was a very, very luxuriant vine.

After I had looked at the tree the missionary told me the story: These great trees in Jamaica grow up in all their grandeur, attain a tremendous stature, and then one day the seed of a little vine, flying through the air, lodges itself in a bit of dirt where one of the tree's branches joins the trunk. The seed takes root there and begins to grow. It commences as a harmless little vine, but as it develops, feeding on the strength and the life of the tree, eventually it becomes greater and stronger than the tree. Finally, the vine is flourishing and the tree is absolutely dead.

When I looked at that tree, I said to myself, "What a very, very vivid picture of the path of sin!" It starts with just a little bit of dirt; a very, very tiny seed is sown. It springs up in some kind of apparently harmless action, but it grows and twists itself around and around the life of a man until, at last, it has almost completely destroyed him. Eventually the sin takes command and the individual is helpless in its grip.

Do not let sin fool you. Remember the story of David, and the experience of thousands of other people—sin usually commences with an incident that is apparently harmless but inevitably terminates with consequences that are appallingly destructive.

The second thing that the story of the scarlet sin of David and Bathsheba tells us about sin is this: *Sin is always discovered eventually*. Let me repeat that. *Sin is always discovered eventually*. I suppose after his affair with Bathsheba, when several weeks or perhaps months had gone by, David came to the conclusion that he had got away with his sin. He had done something that was wrong, but it had been covered up—nobody knew about it, and he would not be exposed.

Then came the fatal message to David from Bathsheba, "David, I am with child!"[1] and immediately the sin that he had thought was hidden was exposed; the sin that had been committed in the darkness of the night, without human knowledge or human witness, was coming to light. The vulture of sin that had been hatched under the cover of darkness had come home to roost on the shoulder of the sinner. That is why the Bible says, "Be sure your sin will find you out."[2]

Sin always, under any circumstance, will eventually be discovered. For years criminals have been in search of the perfect crime, but although they have tried again and again, the person who has had anything to do with criminology will tell you that there is no perfect crime. The criminal always leaves a loop-hole; he makes a mistake, he goes in the wrong direction, or he does some little thing that leaves its track behind him. For centuries now men and women, because they love darkness rather than light, have looked for the perfect sin—the sin they could commit which would never be discovered, but the Bible tells us there is no perfect sin. You cannot get away with sin, no matter how you try.

Your sin will be exposed either here in this world, as was David's, or it will be exposed at the Judgment. Happy is the man whose sin finds him out in this world and he lives to experience repentance and confession and reunion with God, but unhappy, miserable, wretched is the man who gets away with his sin in this world and some day has to stand before God and see his sin exposed.

Which would you prefer? Would you rather it was exposed here while you still have a chance to confess it and make it right, or would you choose to have it hidden here and exposed after it is too late to do anything about it?

[1] 2 Sam. xi. 5.　　　　　[2] Num. xxxii. 23.

G

The final thing that I would like to say about sin is this: *Sin always bears a penalty.*

David experienced something of the penalty for sin. You remember when Nathan, the prophet, came before David he told him the story of a rich man that had stolen a poor man's only lamb. When he asked the king for his judgment in the case David was angry, he was indignant at the rich man, and he declared that the lamb should be restored four-fold, and the man should pay the death penalty. It was then that Nathan turned to David and spoke as only a prophet of God would have the courage to speak, "Thou art the man!"[1]

David had decreed that there should be a four-fold restoration and David himself paid a four-fold penalty for his sin. The baby that was born to Bathsheba as a result of his sin died. He lived to see his own son, Ammon, rape his daughter Tamar. His son Absalom murdered Ammon for the rape of Tamar. Finally, his beloved son Absalom rebelled, took up arms against his own father, threatening his kingdom, and finally, while hanging helplessly by the hair of his head from a tree, Absalom was murdered.

David indeed paid dearly and bitterly for the sin of adultery and murder, but in conclusion this is the thing I want you to notice. Here is the glorious Gospel message of the story: although he paid four-fold for his sin, David was spared the penalty of death. Because he repented and turned to God, trusting in the shed blood of the Messiah that was yet to come, he was forgiven, and did not have to give his life. Although he deserved death, he was pardoned, and Jesus paid the death penalty in David's place.

Shortly after the last great world war a friend of mine visited the psychopathic ward of one of America's great

[1] 2 Sam. xii. 7.

military hospitals. In the course of his visit he stopped to talk to a young man who was lying in bed but appeared to be perfectly normal. As they began their conversation they talked about things in general at first and then the young man began to tell my friend his story.

"I had a buddy by the name of Bill, with whom I served almost continually in the armed forces. We were fortunate enough to be kept together through our entire military career. Everywhere I went he went. We were inseparable. During the course of our army life we became very much attached to one another.

"Of course as we moved from place to place in the fighting zones every once in a while we came into a position of rather acute danger. Usually in such an instance somebody has to make a 'break' for it or venture into some unprotected tract of land, or do something that involves personal danger. In view of this, my buddy and I made a pact between ourselves that whenever such a situation arose where personal danger was involved, we would take turns facing it. One time he would go first; the next time it would be my turn and I would go. That way we divided the peril in half.

"One day we were sitting together in a little ditch which ran along by the side of a roadway. On the ground between the ditch and the roadway there was a hedge. Bill and I were with a reconnoitring party and it was essential that one of us make a 'break' across the roadway. We realized, of course, that there was every possibility that it would be under direct enemy fire and we knew that whoever made the 'break' first would be involved in personal danger.

"As we sat there I realized that it was my turn to take the chance. Bill had gone the last time. I let a few precious moments slip by while I was trying to muster up enough courage to make the 'break.' Just before I was ready to leap out of the trench and through the hedge and across the road, I was startled by the rustle of leaves and then a loud blast, and to my horror and amazement when I looked down at my side where Bill had been I saw the crumpled body of my buddy lying in the trench, covered with blood, his head blown completely off."

The young man in the mental ward of the military hospital turned to my friend as he sat there by his bedside, and in a calm voice at first he said, "You see, sir, the thing that I can never forget is the fact that it was my turn, but Bill took my place."

Then he raised his voice a little bit, "It was my turn, but he took my place."

The next time his voice almost reached a yell as he cried out, "It was my turn, but he took my place. It was my turn, but he took my place."

Then, with a shriek that penetrated through all of the corridors of the hospital, he cried out in dismay and desperation, "It was my turn, but he took my place!"

It took several internes and nurses to hold the young man down in his bed and give him an injection that would quiet his nerves once again. At length, with a final shudder of shame, he lay still.

Many hundreds of years ago now it was David's turn but Jesus Christ took his place. David deserved to die for his sins. He said so himself: but David did not die, even though it was his turn, because Jesus Christ died in his stead.

One day because of my sin I deserved to die. The Bible says, "The wages of sin is death."[1] The Bible says, "The soul that sinneth, it shall die."[2] It was my turn, but I trusted the Lord Jesus Christ as my own personal Saviour, and He took my place.

Perhaps there was a day when you, too, trusted the

[1] Rom. vi. 23.   [2] Ezek. xviii. 4.

Lord Jesus Christ as your own personal Saviour. You realized that you were a sinner—that as a sinner you, too, deserved the death penalty, and you allowed the Lord Jesus Christ to take your place, but this hour finds you like David of old, far away from God because of your sin. You, too, have yielded to some great temptation and allowed sin to gain dominion over you. May I urge you once again to turn in faith to the Lord Jesus Christ in a spirit of confession, repentance, and renunciation, and experience the forgiving grace of God that was such a blessing to David during his latter years.

On the other hand, perhaps you are a complete stranger to the grace of God. Let me remind you of the fact that you are a sinner. The Bible says, "All have sinned, and come short of the glory of God."[1] You, too, deserve the death penalty. You, too, must some day pay that penalty by spending your eternity in total separation from God in hell, unless you yield to the convicting power of the Holy Spirit that is speaking to your heart right now, trust the Lord Jesus Christ as your own personal Saviour, and let Him take your place.

Bearing shame and scoffing rude,
In my place condemned He stood,
Sealed my pardon with His blood;
Hallelujah! What a Saviour!"

[1] Rom. iii. 23.

GOD AND THE ERRING CHILD

FROM THE BIBLE

"A certain man had two sons: And the younger of them said to his father, Father, give me the portion of goods that falleth to me. And he divided unto them his living. And not many days after the younger son gathered all together, and took his journey into a far country, and there wasted his substance with riotous living. And when he had spent all, there arose a mighty famine in that land; and he began to be in want. And he arose and came to his father, But when he was yet a great way off, his father saw him, and had compassion, and ran, and fell on his neck, and kissed him. And the son said unto him, Father, I have sinned against heaven, and in thy sight, and am no more worthy to be called thy son. But the father said to his servants, Bring forth the best robe, and put it on him; and put a ring on his hand, and shoes on his feet: And bring hither the fatted calf, and kill it; and let us eat, and be merry. Now his elder son was in the field: and as he came and drew nigh to the house, he heard musick and dancing. And he called one of the servants, and asked what these things meant. And he said unto him, Thy brother is come; and thy father hath killed the fatted calf, because he hath received him safe and sound. And he was angry, and would not go in: therefore came his father out and intreated him."[1]

[1] Luke xv. 11–14, 20–23, 25–28.

CHAPTER VII

GOD AND THE ERRING CHILD

THE story of the Prodigal Son tells us that there is a way for the erring child to renew his fellowship with God.

There are three different kinds of erring children mentioned in the Bible. There is the apostate. He is the man who has made a false profession of following the Lord Jesus Christ and has finally given it up. The apostate is typified by such men as Judas. Outwardly Judas began to follow Jesus on exactly the same terms as the other disciples, but in the Garden of Gethesmane, as he planted the kiss of betrayal on the Lord's brow, he declared himself to be an apostate. Sad to say, we have many apostates even in our modern Christian churches. We have Judas the elder, Judas the deacon, Judas the preacher, and sometimes even Judas the missionary.

The apostate is the kind of person that John was speaking about when he said, "They went out from us, but they were not of us; for if they had been of us, they would no doubt have continued with us: but they went out, that they might be made manifest that they were not all of us."[1]

Then there is the child of God who has slipped into some form of open sin or worldliness. In the Bible he is typified by such men as David and Peter—both of them undoubtedly sincere in their faith but weak in the flesh.

Finally, there is the Christian who has not fallen into

[1] 1 John ii. 19.

open sin but who has lost ground spiritually in some measure. He is typified by Thomas, the disciple. "Doubting Thomas" was not a great sinner but he had deteriorated spiritually from the man he was when he had been willing to deny himself, take up his cross, and follow Jesus.

The story of the father and son in Luke's Gospel gives us a very beautiful picture of God. It is quite true that in many places in the Bible God is visualized as hard, severe, vindictive, righteous, and without feeling. But in the story of the Prodigal Son we see an entirely different aspect of the nature of God. We see Him as a father—kind, loving, lenient, gentle, long-suffering, and patient. Until we know God not only as righteous and vindictive, but also as fatherly and loving, we have failed to see the Bible picture of God.

In the story we learn five things about God and the erring child.

The erring child is quite often one who has been in close fellowship with God.

Obviously the father in the story had only two sons. The Bible speaks of the Prodigal as the "younger." If there had been more the word "youngest" would have been used. This means that the boy in the story was the baby in the family, and although the eldest son usually stands first as far as inheritance is concerned, everyone knows that the baby in any family always stands first when it comes to love and affection. Normally it is the baby who is spoiled, if anyone is spoiled. In most families he is able to get far more out of his father than any other member of the family. He usually holds a place of affection and favouritism that the other children do not have.

This would mean that the Prodigal was actually closer to his father personally than was the elder son. In all probability if the other boy had come with the same petition of dividing the inheritance ahead of time, he would have been refused flatly, but because the father loved the younger son so much he weakened and responded to his request. This, then, is the story of a son who was very close, personally, to his father deliberately wandering a great distance from his father. It was the father's favourite who became the erring child.

The outstanding example of backsliding in the Old Testament is the story of David, but strangely enough, the story of David is also the account of a man who was probably closer to God than any other one character in the Old Testament. The Bible tells us that David was a man after God's own heart. He was a spiritual giant among Old Testament characters and yet he fell into the debauchery of murder and adultery.

In the New Testament the outstanding example of an erring child is the story of the Apostle Peter, and again it is the story of a man who was in close fellowship with the Lord and drifted a great distance from the Lord. I believe Peter was probably in closer personal contact with Jesus Christ than any of the other disciples. He was always the most aggressive. He seemed to be the most devoted. He was the only one who dared to walk on the water or to defend Jesus in the Garden of Gethsemane. He was there a great many times when no one else was there. He was one of the three on the Mount of Transfiguration and one of the three who followed Jesus the farthest into the garden. However, strange though it may seem, this man who was closer to Jesus than any of the other disciples became the erring child.

It is the one who has gone up a long way that can fall down the farthest. Extreme contrasts in life often lie very close to one another. The musician knows that there is just a hair's breadth between discord and harmony—one note can make all the difference in the world. Psychologists tell us that there is a very thin line between the genius and the demented, and the Bible makes it very clear that in one sense at least it is not very far from the greatness of spirituality to the gutter of sin. That is why the Bible says, "Let him that thinketh he standeth take heed lest he fall."[1] The erring child is quite often one who has been in close fellowship with God.

The erring child does not plunge into open sin and worldliness all at once.

It took a long time and it was a great distance from the wealth and fellowship of the father's house to the wretchedness and famine of the foreign country. There were a great many miles and a great many circumstances between the two. That is why we usually refer to the erring child as a backslider. We do not call him the "back-runner", or the "back-jumper". The way down is long, hard, and slow.

Have you ever noticed how the roadway winds down the side of a mountain? As you drive down in your car the road twists and turns so much you are almost unaware of the fact that you are descending, but after you have driven for half an hour along comparatively gradual slopes and then look back up, you see how far down you have come without realizing it.

The road into the far country starts with temptation, the temptation becomes a thought, the thought becomes a desire of the heart, the desire of the heart becomes a secretive act, and at length the secretive act becomes an open sin.

The erring child does not plunge into open sin and worldliness all at once.

The erring child usually goes through two stages in the far country.

[1] I Cor. x. 12.

At first the backslider is *indifferent* to his condition. If you read the story in Luke and stop at verse thirteen, you will see the Prodigal in the far country, out of fellowship with his father, but entirely indifferent to his own condition. He was still spending his substance in riotous living, he was having a good time, he was getting a thrill out of life, and he looked for sympathy from no one.

If you were to have approached him at this point in his wandering, you would have found him filled with excuses that seemed perfectly logical in his own mind as to why he had left his father's home. Most prominent among his excuses would probably have been his elder brother. Obviously the two boys did not get along very well, because even after the Prodigal returned the elder son was jealous and embittered because his father treated him so well. This feeling had probably been there throughout their lives, even as boys, and when the temptation of the far country came into the mind of the younger son he used his brother's maltreatment as his excuse for breaking the heart of his father.

Usually there is a stage in the wanderings of every backslider when he lays the blame upon some Christian who has mistreated him, perhaps an official in the church, or even the pastor. As long as he blames it upon some other person he will be indifferent to his own need and to the longing of his Father God for his return.

At the end of verse thirteen, the Prodigal did not see his father's broken heart nor did he understand his longing for the return of his beloved son. He was not moved by the fact that he had caused his father's hair to turn grey. He was hard, cynical, and indifferent. He had plenty of money left and he still had his brother to blame.

If in the midst of his indifference the modern backslider could only see that he has used the maltreatment of some Christian as an excuse for turning his back upon a God who has never let him down, I am convinced that he would think seriously about returning. That is why God turned to the children of Israel in the midst of their backsliding and said, "Thus saith the Lord, What iniquity have your fathers found in *me*, that they are gone far from me? For my people have committed two evils; they have forsaken me the fountain of living waters, and have hewed them out cisterns, broken cisterns, that can hold no water."[1]

The glamour of the far country and the sensual thrill of riotous living has blinded the eyes of the erring child to the fact that he has forsaken a father who loves him a great deal and he is blaming it upon a Christian who does not love him at all. He has given up the real comfort and security of his fellowship with God for the fake and false security of the world, the flesh and the devil. He has turned his back upon the cistern that is filled to the brim with living water and has embraced broken cisterns that can hold no water.

Perhaps you are at this stage in your wanderings from God—still satisfied with the world, bitter against God, and completely indifferent to your own need spiritually. Would to God that you could realize that although Christians may have let you down, God has never forsaken you. Christians may have broken their promises, but God has always been faithful to His Word. Do not blame God for what other people have done to you. Do not forsake God because you feel that the organized church has forsaken you. Do not sacrifice permanent fellowship and communion with God on the altar of immediate frivolity in the far country.

To the end of verse thirteen the Prodigal Son is indifferent, but from the beginning of verse fourteen to the

[1] Jer. ii. 5, 13.

end of the story he becomes exceedingly *anxious*. "He had spent all . . . and he began to be in want."[1]

The erring child may be indifferent to God and his own condition for many years but eventually the time will come when he will be anxious. He may pursue the bubble of sin for a season but some day the bubble will break. There is joy in the world, but it is temporary. There is satisfaction in the far country, but it is limited. There are thrills in the service of Satan, but not indefinitely. The world's river of joy always empties into a pool of tears. The wells of satisfaction in the far country inevitably turn bitter. The waves of thrill in the service of Satan will eventually dash the erring child against the rocks of misery and despair.

There was a time when the Prodigal lived riotously, but there was also a time when he began to be in want. In verse fourteen he is sick of his sin and wandering and anxious for the fellowship and the blessing and the security of his father's home. "How many hired servants of my father's have bread enough and to spare, and I perish with hunger!"[2] The erring child goes through two stages—indifference and anxiety.

When the erring child returns to his father he is not scolded for his sin but is welcomed with open arms and forgiven with a kiss of love.

The account says the father *ran* to meet the son. He ran lest his son change his mind and go back to the far country. He ran lest his son fall of exhaustion by the wayside and fail to complete his journey. He ran lest some new evil overtake him before he reached the shelter of his father's home.

And that is the way God welcomes the return of His erring child. When the backslider starts for God, God starts for the backslider.

[1] Luke xv. 14.   [2] Luke xv. 17.

Not only did the father run to meet his son, when he reached him he kissed him. He did not scold him for his wandering and his sin. He knew that the far country had taken its toll and inflicted its own penalty. The boy had long since lost his money and his friends, he had been lowered to the position of a swineherd, and when he came home his clothing was tattered and torn and worn and his own mind was bewildered, confused, and upset. Sin had left its marks; there was no need for further scolding.

The modern backslider is in exactly the same condition. Very seldom is there need for scolding and rebuke upon the part of the children of God. The wanderer has already paid the penalty of a dissipated body or a tormented mind, and within his heart there is a longing for fellowship with the children of God and reunion with God Himself. He does not need a rebuke, he needs a reception. He does not need to be chided, he needs to be comforted. The father in the story knew this and so he ran and fell on his neck and kissed him.

Not so with the elder brother. He was suspicious and jealous. He doubted the reality of the wanderer's repentance, and he would much rather have held him at arm's length or kept him in the position of an outcast than have received him as warmly and lovingly as did his father.

Many Christian people rejoice at the return of the backslider and do everything within their power to welcome him, love him, and make it easy for him to renew his fellowship; but, sad to say, the erring child often returns to the Church of Jesus Christ and finds it besmirched with elder brothers—men who have such an unearthly sense of spiritual superiority that they feel they are in a position to doubt the reality of another's sincerity.

As I read my Bible I am thoroughly convinced that it is not for us to question the reality of the erring child's repentance but it is our business to forgive him as God forgives him and take him under the shelter of our wing as quickly as possible, praying God to keep both him and us from ever falling again.

But what about his sin? questions the man who has been fortunate enough, by the grace of God, to have resisted temptation. If sin is confessed it is under the blood to be remembered against him no more. We are not naturally any better than the backslider, but the mercy of God has protected us, and but for the grace of God we might all be in exactly the same position as the erring child.

Oh how many wanderers there are who live within a stone's throw of the fellowship of Christian people in a Christian church but who are separated from that fellowship by a vast desert of criticism, gossip, and self-righteousness among people that are in the church! Undoubtedly some day these people will have to reckon with God and they will be held responsible for their actions.

When the erring child returns, it is usually to a place of greater blessing, sweeter communion, and more active service.

The Prodigal Son was given a robe because he had been forgiven for his wandering. A ring was placed upon his finger because his father considered him a member of the family. Shoes were put upon his feet because now he could be of service to the family. The fatted calf was killed because now he was able to enjoy the blessings of the family, and finally a banquet was prepared because he was again to experience the satisfaction and joy of living in fellowship with the family.

His position after his return from the far country was in many ways superior to his position before he had left home.

And so it is with the backslider. He is forgiven for his sin and robed in the righteousness of the Son of God.

H

His heavenly Father has welcomed him and restored him to a position of good standing in the family of God. His feet are shod anew with the preparation of the Gospel of peace, and now, more than ever, he can be of service to his Saviour. The blessings of God as a fatted calf are spread before him and all the resources of Heaven are available to him, and after years of wandering he thrills again to that joy which is "unspeakable and full of glory."[1] After the misery, the want, and the unrest of the far country he is bathed again in the peace of God which passeth understanding.

[1] I Pet. i. 8.

CHAPTER VIII

THE WAY TO GOD

FROM THE BIBLE

"Now faith is the substance of things hoped for, the evidence of things not seen. For by it the elders obtained a good report. Through faith we understand that the worlds were framed by the word of God, so that things which are seen were not made of things which do appear. By faith Abel offered unto God a more excellent sacrifice than Cain, by which he obtained witness that he was righteous, God testifying of his gifts: and by it he being dead yet speaketh. By faith Enoch was translated that he should not see death; and was not found, because God had translated him: for before his translation he had this testimony, that he pleased God. But without faith it is impossible to please him: for he that cometh to God must believe that he is, and that he is a rewarder of them that diligently seek him."[1]

[1] Heb. xi. 1–6.

CHAPTER VIII

THE WAY TO GOD

NO one has ever succeeded in proving scientifically that God exists.

As long as men have lived in this world they have used their intellect, their logic, and, in recent years, their scientific method to prove theoretically that God actually exists. Many a person believes that if he is to have any contact with God he must first of all prove the existence of God. However, all of the philosophers, theologians, and scientists have failed in their attempts. No one has ever proved, scientifically, the existence of God, and from the very nature of the problem we may conclude that no one will ever do so.

Down through the history of man there have been a great many futile attempts. Man has called his attempts proofs. However, a close analysis of his proofs will indicate that they fail logically and do not stand up under scientific testing. Most of the classical proofs for God's existence have long Greek names which we do not understand—cosmological, teleological, ontological, etc. It would take too much time, however, to wade through each of these. Let one be an example, the cosmological proof. It is the best known and perhaps the simplest.

Briefly, the argument is as follows: (1) There is in operation in this world a law of "cause and effect." (2) Such a law leads us to assume that there is a first cause. (3) The first cause is the God of the Bible.

Anyone with an analytical mind can find the flaws in this argument without difficulty. In the first place although the existence of the law of "cause and effect" seems obvious, no one has ever proved that there actually is such a law in operation. The famous English philosopher, David Hume, brought out this point explicitly, and although in this connection he did not make much positive progress, he did manage to point out the negative aspect of the problem, namely, that it is impossible to prove cause and effect.

In the second place, if we were to admit the existence of such a law there is no necessity of a first cause. The alternative to a first cause would be an infinite regression of causes, just as there is an infinite regression of the number series in pure mathematics.

Finally, even if we admit the first two premises—that there is a law of cause and effect and there is a first cause—there is no need to conclude that the first cause is the God of the Bible. We might describe the first cause with any one of a dozen names that are used by the philosophers—impersonal force, supreme will, atomic energy, absolute mind, or pure reason. We are not bound to come to the conclusion that if there is a first cause it must be the God of the Bible.

Thus this scientific proof of man breaks down in each of its three premises, and if we had time at our disposal we could go on to show how all of the other so-called proofs that man has put forth for the existence of God also break down. It is absolutely impossible for anybody to prove, scientifically, that God exists.

The reason is obvious: man can only deal scientifically with non-spiritual things. In order to prove anything he must be able in some way to demonstrate it. The Bible tells us that God is not material but spiritual. How can a materialist apprehend the existence of a spiritual God?

It is absolutely impossible. The Bible teaches us quite clearly that the unregenerate man has no spiritual perception and thus can know nothing of spiritual things. "But the natural man receiveth not the things of the Spirit of God: for they are foolishness unto him: neither can he know them, because they are spiritually discerned."[1]

"But what about my own personal experience with God? I talk with Him every morning. He is with me throughout the day. I commune with Him before I sleep at night. Does not this prove that God exists?"

Certainly, you may thank God that you do know Him personally, and there are thousands of other Christians who can say exactly the same thing. Remember, however, your personal experience does prove that God exists, but only for you. My personal experience of God proves God's existence, but only for me. The fact that you and I know God does not prove His existence to unregenerate man. He has only our word for it, and that does not constitute an objective scientific proof.

So then we must conclude that it is not only useless, but absolutely impossible, to apply the methods of science in an attempt to establish our belief in the existence of God, or in any of the other Christian doctrines.

In this connection we must also remember that the existence of God cannot be disproved by the methods of science. Since the natural man cannot deal with spiritual things, it is just as foolish for him to try to prove that God does *not* exist as it is for him to try to prove that God does exist.

This fact may be useful to the ardent Christian at times when he is attempting to defend his faith. If he is backed into a corner by someone who insists that he should be able to prove that God exists, he will find that he can turn the tables completely by asking his adversary to prove

[1] 1 Cor. ii. 14.

that God does *not* exist.   Both propositions are impossible to prove by the ordinary methods of science.

Signposts to God

Although we cannot prove scientifically that God exists, we would be blind indeed if we did not realize that in this world there are a great many signposts that point in the direction of God. The world is filled with signposts to God but there are no signposts away from God that cannot be adequately explained.

The Word of God says, "The heavens declare the glory of God."[1] The heavens do not prove God's existence, but as we look at the sky on a clear night and see the myriad of stars shedding their light upon the world, as we glory in the golden path of the harvest moon, and as we bask under the brilliance of the summer sun, our hearts naturally respond and say, "God!"

The stars do not prove the existence of God, scientifically, but as each little star twinkles in the Milky Way it is crying out to the entire world, "God—in that direction." The brilliance of the moon as it sheds its silver path across a glassy stretch of water does not prove the existence of God, but it does cry out in a slightly louder voice, "God—in that direction."

When the sun breaks through a pile of clouds that it has lined with silver and sheds its warmth and vitality upon a dead piece of ground, calling it to life and growth and beauty, it does not prove the existence of God, but in a thunderous voice it is crying out, "God—in that direction!"

The earth declares the glory of God. "For the invisible things of him from the creation of the world are clearly seen, being understood by the things that are made,

[1] Ps. xix. 1.

even his eternal power and Godhead; so that they are without excuse."[1] Let our eyes move from the heavens to the earth and there are still signposts on every hand pointing in the direction of God.

The man who picks up a watch on the seashore automatically concludes that somebody made it. It is very unlikely that an instrument so delicate and so perfectly formed could have come into existence by chance. If there is a watch there is usually a watch-maker. The existence of the watch does not prove, scientifically, that there is a watch-maker. There is the bare, and almost ridiculous possibility that the watch came into existence by a coincidence of circumstances. However, the average intelligent person would come to the conclusion that the watch pointed in the direction of a watch-maker.

The Bible tells us that all along the seashores of life there are watches, and every watch points in the direction of its Maker. Every flower, every bush, and every tree is a watch. The animals that roam through the jungles, the fish that swim in the sea, and the insects that crawl across the dirt, are watches. The air we breathe, the minerals we dig from the bowels of the earth, and the wonders of nature are watches.

They do not prove the existence of God. There is the bare possibility that they could have come into existence by some chance of circumstance. There is the possibility that they might have been the result of an impersonal force. However, the most probable conclusion is that God created them. In their own way and in their own place they are crying out exactly what the stars, the moon, and the sun are saying: "God—in that direction!"

Suppose a man is driving down the highway and he wants to go to a certain city. After a while he sees a signpost that tells him the city is in the opposite direction.

[1] Rom. i. 20.

He ignores the sign and drives on. At length he sees another sign post that tells him the city is the other way. He ignores this second sign also and drives on. Finally, he sees a third sign which points in the opposite direction and indicates that the city is behind him. Instead of turning around and going the direction the signs point, he concludes that someone has made a mistake. The signs are there by accident. They are pointing in the wrong direction. He is right and the signs are wrong. And so he goes on—mile after mile—passing sign after sign, and all of them declare that the city to which he wishes to go is in the opposite direction, but he ignores them all and drives on.

"That man," you say, "is a fool! Any individual that would deliberately drive down a highway and ignore all the signposts is a fool."

And that is exactly why the Bible says, "The fool hath said in his heart there is no God."[1]

The heavens do not prove the existence of God. The world does not prove the existence of God, but they are signposts on the highway of life that point in the direction of God. The man who ignores the signposts and goes on in his own way, refusing to believe in God, is a fool.

If we cannot prove the existence of God scientifically, but the signposts point definitely in the direction of God, how can we know God?

Faith

That question can be answered in one word—FAITH. Faith is the only way to God. If you are not willing to believe in God by faith, then you will never know anything about Him. The Word of God is filled with it. Faith is God's way to spiritual perception.

[1] Ps. xiv. 1.

It may come as rather a surprise to the average Christian but nevertheless it is true: God never expected anyone to prove that He exists. As a matter of fact, I believe that God would be displeased should anyone succeed in doing so, because God Himself has established this unalterable law: that the relation between man and Himself must be one of faith, not of rational proof. "But without faith it is impossible to please God; for he that cometh to God must believe that he is, and that he is the rewarder of them that diligently seek him."[1]

Christianity dependent upon faith

Not only is it a fact that we cannot prove with the methods of science that God exists, but, astounding as it may seem, this very fact is the bulwark of Christianity's foundation. Even a casual glance through the Bible will prove conclusively that the fundamental principle of Christianity is faith. Faith is the rock upon which it stands. "For in Jesus Christ neither circumcision availeth anything, nor uncircumcision; but faith which worketh by love. For whatsoever is born of God overcometh the world: and this is the victory that overcometh the world, even our faith."[2]

Victory over the world is not gained through our intellectual proofs, or our reasoning powers, or the scientific method. Victory over the world is accomplished through faith.

Suppose that someone should find a conclusive theoretical proof for the existence of God. Most people would consider such a proof cause for great rejoicing. Not so. It would be cause for grave anxiety and concern, for it would be injurious to Christianity. Why? Simply because it would lead someone to build on the sands of

[1] Heb. xi. 6.   [2] Gal. v. 6; 1 John v. 4.

reason rather than the rock of faith. It would damage the foundation of Christianity, for where there is proof there is no need of faith. The very definition of faith excludes the necessity of proof. Once the existence of anything is proved conclusively, it is not necessary to believe in it by faith.

If we rest our claims upon theoretical proofs, as so many do, these will always be subject to attack and to the possibility of refutation. But, when we realize that our cause does not rest upon any system of reasoning and proof, but on faith, then we stand upon a foundation that can never be shaken.

What is faith?

Does the average man ever exercise it? Did anyone ever come to know God by it? Is it completely irrational, or has it any basis in reason?

The Bible tells us that "Faith is the substance of things hoped for, the evidence of things not seen."[1] To believe in God by faith means to believe without the use of any of our five senses. Faith is believing in spite of the absence of proof.

In almost every sphere of life, faith is essential. The farmer plants his seed in the spring or fall, and then he goes away and does some other work on his farm. However, long before there is any sign of a crop, he plans for the harvest. He hires men and trucks. He overhauls his machinery. His wife lays in a store of food for the harvesters. The barns are cleared of last year's crop, and the grain bins are prepared. But what for? There is no crop as yet. The field looks like any other cultivated area. Why all the preparation? The farmer *believes* that there is going to be a crop. He cannot see it. The ground is bare. But he believes it will come. And how? Simply

[1] Heb. xi. 1.

by faith in the processes of nature. Without faith the farmer could not operate.

I am sure you remember your first days at school. One day the teacher told you that in 1492 Columbus sailed from Spain and landed in the West Indies. Undoubtedly you believed that story when the teacher told it, but you were not there when Columbus landed. You did not see his three ships as they hove into sight of land, and yet, even now, you believe all of it. Why? Because you had faith in the teacher's word. You had faith in your history book. If you take time to think about it, you will discover that it is impossible to learn anything without exercising faith—faith in a man's word, faith in a book, faith in the label on a bottle. Education is dependent upon faith.

So it is with any phase of life. Wherever you go and whatever you do, faith is essential.

In the eleventh chapter of the Book of Hebrews we find a long list of men whom God honoured, and we notice that everyone of them came to God, believed in God, and knew God by faith. "By faith Noah——" obeyed God and built an ark that proved the salvation of himself and his household. "By faith Abraham——" left his own land and went out to another place, "not knowing whither he went."

Faith has always been the only way to know God, and faith is still the only way to know God.

Is faith reasonable?

Faith is every bit as reasonable as is the scientific method. The boast of the average scientist is this: "I will not accept anything on such a flimsy basis as faith. Everything that I believe must be proved."

Although the average scientist does not admit it, he exercises just as much faith as the Christian. The

Christian puts his faith in God, whereas the scientist puts his faith in his own sense perception and reasoning powers. He trusts the conclusions at which he arrives by the use of his own intellect. And that is nothing more than faith —faith in his mind.

It is not very difficult to show the weakness of such a position. Science is great but it is not infallible.

The many cases of optical illusion should be sufficient to prove that the findings of our senses are not always conclusive proof of anything. The very progress of science itself through the years proves that the human reason has never been entirely infallible. If it were infallible, the scientists would never have come to any wrong conclusions, but history has proved that they have been absolutely wrong many times and have had to discard beliefs that had been formulated by reason and held for years.

In view of this, is it any more reasonable for the rationalist or the scientist to put his faith in his reasoning powers, or sense perception, than it is for the Christian to put his faith in God? Both positions assume faith in something.

The necessity of action

We have concluded that God may be known by faith and faith alone. Faith is the way to God. I have attempted to define faith. I have pointed out the place of faith in everyday life and have shown that faith in God is quite reasonable.

Thus I may have succeeded in convincing you that the Christian position is strong, and you may wish with all your heart to know God. But you must realize that no matter what your convictions may be, unless you act upon them you will never know God.

There must be a time when you take the step of faith

that will bring you into a personal relationship with God. The electric-light switch will illuminate a dark room—but only when it is turned on. Being convinced of the fact will not turn on the lights. Turning the switch will. Action is absolutely necessary.

No one will ever prove scientifically that God exists, but remember that all of the signposts of life point in the direction of God, and you can know God through faith.

Have you ever turned the switch of faith? You can never know God until you do so. Argument is useless unless it results in action. "Blessed are they that have not seen, and yet have believed."[1]

[1] John xx. 29.